Learn Apple HomeKit on iOS

A Home Automation Guide for Developers, Designers, and Homeowners

Jesse Feiler

Apress®

Learn Apple HomeKit on iOS: A Home Automation Guide for Developers, Designers, and Homeowners

Jesse Feiler
Plattsburgh, New York
USA

ISBN-13 (pbk): 978-1-4842-1528-9   ISBN-13 (electronic): 978-1-4842-1527-2
DOI 10.1007/978-1-4842-1527-2

Library of Congress Control Number: 2016960323

Managing Director: Welmoed Spahr
Lead Editor: Aaron Black
Technical Reviewer: Aaron Crabtree
Editorial Board: Steve Anglin, Pramila Balan, Laura Berendson, Aaron Black, Louise Corrigan, Jonathan Gennick, Robert Hutchinson, Celestin Suresh John, Nikhil Karkal, James Markham, Susan McDermott, Matthew Moodie, Natalie Pao, Gwenan Spearing
Coordinating Editor: Jessica Vakili
Copy Editor: Lori Jacobs
Compositor: SPi Global
Indexer: SPi Global
Artist: SPi Global

Distributed to the book trade worldwide by Springer Science+Business Media New York, 233 Spring Street, 6th Floor, New York, NY 10013. Phone 1-800-SPRINGER, fax (201) 348-4505, e-mail orders-ny@springer-sbm.com, or visit www.springeronline.com. Apress Media, LLC is a California LLC and the sole member (owner) is Springer Science + Business Media Finance Inc (SSBM Finance Inc). SSBM Finance Inc is a **Delaware** corporation.

For information on translations, please e-mail rights@apress.com or visit www.apress.com.

Apress and friends of ED books may be purchased in bulk for academic, corporate, or promotional use. eBook versions and licenses are also available for most titles. For more information, reference our Special Bulk Sales–eBook Licensing web page at www.apress.com/bulk-sales.

Any source code or other supplementary materials referenced by the author in this text are available to readers at www.apress.com. For detailed information about how to locate your book's source code, go to www.apress.com/source-code/. Readers can also access source code at SpringerLink in the Supplementary Material section for each chapter.

Printed on acid-free paper

Contents at a Glance

Contents

About the Author

Jesse Feiler Jesse Feiler helps people and organizations get to know and use new technologies. Projects have included building the page caching module for the Prodigy Web Browser for Mac in the very early days of the Web, location-based apps for iPhone and iOS, as well as books and classes on new technologies. Recent books include *iPad For Seniors for Dummies* (9th ed.) and *Learn Apple HomeKit for iOS*.

Current projects involve using apps and FileMaker databases for identifying and managing risk in nonprofit organizations as well as helping small communities build location-based apps to promote tourism, downtown economic development, and the wise use of natural resources.

He is founder and president of Friends of Saranac River Trail (saranacrivertrail.org) whose flagship events are the annual Talks, Treks & Tasks which include treks to the Plattsburgh Water Pollution Control Plant, treks focusing on edible plants along the trail as well as invasive species, and talks on current issues in trail and path design and development.

Born in Washington, DC, Jesse currently lives in Plattsburgh, NY, where this book was written.

For more information on development as well as updates to this book, visit Jesse's web site at northcountryconsulting.com. For information on his apps and app consulting, visit champlainarts.com.

About the Technical Reviewer

Aaron Crabtree A passionate developer and experience enthusiast, Aaron Crabtree has been involved in mobile development since the dawn of the mobile device. He has written and provided technical editing for a variety of books on the topic, as well as taken the lead on some very cool, cutting-edge projects over the years. His latest endeavor, building apps for augmented reality devices, has flung him back where he wants to be: as an early adopter in an environment that changes day by day as new innovation hits the market. Hit him up on Twitter where he tweets about all things mobile and AR: @aaron_crabtree.

Acknowledgments

As always, thanks to Carole Jelen at Waterside Productions. Aaron Crabtree has once again provided great help in the technical issues of an Apple technology. At Apress, Jessica Vakili and Aaron Black have been invaluable in helping to bring this book into being.

Introduction

HomeKit is something new from Apple. Something really new. It's not a new device like an iPhone, an iPad, or even the Mac itself. And it's not a new app like Pages, Keynote, or even Xcode, the heavy-duty app that is used by Apple and third-party developers to build apps as well as the operating systems themselves (macOS, iOS, tvOS, and now watchOS). HomeKit is basically a data management framework that manages home automation. It joins Apple's HealthKit, which is another data management framework that focuses on health.

There's a pattern here. Apple is bringing its massive resources to a targeted database and framework in the expectation that third-party developers of software and hardware will gather around the framework. It's no coincidence that HomeKit actually runs on the Apple iOS devices: as the HomeKit ecosystem grows, more and more people use it and appreciate the ease of use that comes with most of what Apple touches. The HomeKit framework is designed to support accessories such as lamps, doors and their locks, thermostats, sensors, and the other automated components of a home for the 21st century. And the fact that this flexible and powerful framework just happens to run on the Apple devices is a great incentive for Apple to have built it and to build it in such a way that it is robust enough to handle yet-undreamed-of devices from developers and vendors around the world.

The architecture of a framework such as HomeKit (and HealthKit) is such that there's a relatively modest investment of skill and time needed to extend and customize it for all of the third-party accessories that integrate with it. This is one way of whittling away at the enormous backlog of code that needs to be written to bring the benefits of modern technology to as many people as possible.

This book provides you with two introductions to HomeKit. In the first chapters, you'll see how to set up HomeKit in your home and how to manage your home's *accessories*, *rooms*, and *scenes* (those everyday terms are used in HomeKit's vocabulary with their everyday meanings).

In the second part of the book, you'll see how the point-and-tap commands from the first part of the book can be reimplemented in code so that you can build your own HomeKit apps that combine the components of HomeKit in new and different ways.

As we move into this new type of technology (the kits of frameworks and data management), you can use HomeKit as your entrée to gain experience with a new way of working with technology. If you're not particularly interested in how the software development world is changing with these kits, feel welcome: you can use HomeKit to manage your home's rooms, scenes, and accessories.

Managing your home in this way can make your life easier, but it also can pay off. Deciding when lights and appliances are used helps you create a comfortable home that does not waste electricity and may even manage the use of electricity in such a way as to take advantage of off-peak lower pricing.

It's time to get started.

Chapter 1

Bringing Home Automation Home

If you're used to buying a product like an iPhone, taking it home, turning it on, and getting to work, HomeKit will be a very different experience. HomeKit is an integration technology that brings together your home, HomeKit-enabled accessories (door locks, light bulbs, sensors, and the like), and your own ideas about how your home should be automated.

This chapter provides an introduction to these components and concepts so that you get an idea of what it means to automate your home with HomeKit as well as how you might go about it. Don't worry if it seems as if there are many moving parts to this machine—there are, but HomeKit can help you put them together.

Use the first chapters in this book to get a sense of what is possible. You may want to experiment with devices that you have as you go along, but if you haven't set up a HomeKit home before (or any home automation home at all), don't expect to perform a miracle right away.

That said, HomeKit is a terrific tool to work with once you get the idea of how it works. That basic idea of how it works is the heart of these first few chapters. You may come back to them periodically, but once the proverbial light goes on (not your HomeKit light bulb but the light in your head), you'll see how it works together and how it can—literally—change your life and your home.

© Jesse Feiler 2016

J. Feiler, *Learn Apple HomeKit on iOS*, DOI 10.1007/978-1-4842-1527-2_1

Welcome Home

Projects at Apple (and everywhere else in the technology world) don't happen overnight. Often, they take shape gradually as engineers and users experiment with new ideas and technologies. Many times, a new product's evolution is dependent on one, more, or many outside factors. (Just think of how many technologies went into the first iPhone). HomeKit is a project that brings together a number of technologies not all of which are under Apple's control. The story begins in 2014, but we'll skip to the critical moment at Apple's World Wide Developers Conference (WWDC) in 2016 when Home App was first shown to the public (at least that part of the public that comprises developers and the technology media).

"Internet of Things" (often referred to as IoT) is one of those phrases that floats around for a while and then starts popping up everywhere as if it were something brand new. Before long (well, not *too* long), it seems as if it has always been with us. Apple's HomeKit project was announced in June 2014 at Apple's WWDC. Unlike announcements of Apple products, there was nothing for consumers to rush out and buy. What was available (to developers only) was an API (application program interface—the blueprint for code that developers would start writing to develop with HomeKit). There were some early devices, but not much beyond that.

Then, HomeKit went quiet for a while.

2015: Apple Unveils New Technologies

Although HomeKit was fairly quiet, Apple engineers and third party developers were busily at work.

CarPlay Revs Up

Meanwhile, in another part of Apple's busy campus, engineers were hard at work on CarPlay which had first been announced a year before HomeKit at WWDC in 2013 as iOS in the Car. Early implementations on some models began soon after the announcement. At an event in March 2015, Chief Executive Officer (CEO) Tim Cook announced that CarPlay would be available on vehicles from all the major manufacturers by the end of that year. Sure enough, as the new lines of 2016 models started to hit the showrooms in the fall of 2015, CarPlay was available on many of them.

Although some of the early CarPlay implementations were on high-end cars, the rollout was across a wide range of vehicles as this quiet project suddenly (after only several years of development!) moved front and center. CarPlay lets you integrate your data with your car so that you can listen to your music, use Siri to update or query your calendar, and otherwise bring your digital life with you no matter where you're traveling (provided there's an Internet connection).

Turning On Apple TV

In yet another part of the Apple campus, engineers and designers were plugging away at Apple TV, turning what had been described as a "hobby" for Apple into a new way of thinking about television. In the announcement of Apple TV at the beginning of September 2015, CEO Tim Cook said, "The future of television is apps." That sentence was repeated many times in the course of the presentations at that time. The key point is that television has been a linear medium: you turn it on and watch a show that has a beginning and end. For archived or recorded shows, you play them and watch them—perhaps from beginning to end and perhaps jumping around with fast forward and reverse. No matter how you watch traditional television, it's a linear process.

Apps are inherently nonlinear. You jump into an app and do what you want, and then you jump out to do something else that may be in another app, on another device, and even something unrelated such as going for a walk, having a meal, or discussing something with friends or colleagues.

Watching the Time

The Apple event in March 2015 at which the CarPlay announcement was made was focused on Apple Watch.

Putting It Together

You may be wondering why a book on HomeKit starts by talking about CarPlay, Apple TV, and Apple Watch as well as HomeKit. The answer is simple: it's all part of the same thing. It's a new way of working, playing, learning, and going about your life. Apple's implementation of IoT isn't one thing over here and another over there. What Apple is doing now is what it does best: it is integrating products (its own as well as products from others). Along with the integration, it's simplifying a total picture so that it makes useful sense. As many people have pointed out, Apple tends not to be an innovator in technology. Its forte is innovating in the use of technology and its integration into our lives so that new technology becomes something we can't imagine how we lived without.

This book shows you how to work with HomeKit as a developer of HomeKit-compatible apps, a maker of devices, or an integrator of home automation technologies (a contractor, architect, or designer), or as a user of HomeKit devices who wants to delve deeper into the issues and technologies that just get things working. The focus is on HomeKit, but from time to time you may see how the HomeKit structure shows up in CarPlay and Apple Watch, particularly in the design patterns in the software that are extraordinarily message- and event-driven rather than linear. This shouldn't be surprising, because Apple is just as aware as you are that someone can pay attention to the tap on the wrist from the Apple Watch that reminds him or her that it's time to leave work to drive home for that dinner party. Turning into the driveway on an autumn evening with the early evening settling in, it's reassuring to see the HomeKit lights turn on in the house. If it's starting to snow, it's definitely nice not to have to get out of the car to open the garage door (thanks to HomeKit). Not everything is automated in this little scenario. The dog barks a welcome so you don't want to dally in the car even though you're listening to some music you like. As you open the door, the music follows you from car to your speakers in the house. It's a nice welcoming scenario, and the dog's wagging tail may suggest that he had something to do with it all and please give him a biscuit.

HomeKit, CarPlay, Apple Watch. . . . Yes, you can think of them as great examples of the Internet of Things. What Apple has been thinking about is how they all fit together in your life. We are moving away from a world of huge monolithic apps into one in which small components of apps fit together. So if you're expecting to learn how to build a big "killer" HomeKit app in this book, tamp down your expectation. What you'll build for HomeKit are targeted small apps that fit together within the HomeKit framework. If the user winds up assembling those pieces into a "killer" and convenient home, that's just fine, but what we developers do today is build the pieces that make it possible for users to put together their technology their way.

As noted in the Introduction, the first part of this book (Chapters 1 through 3) provides you with background of the technology and ideas behind it. Then, in Chapters 4 and 5, we'll move on to the details of implementation and the use of HomeKit, focusing on how you can use it yourself. Finally, in Chapters 6 through 9, you'll see how to write code that performs the manual tasks you did in the previous chapters.

If you want to jump ahead, feel free to do so, but make sure to come back to these introductory chapters. They will help you to understand what you have to do in the later ones. Otherwise, it may seem like a collection of unrelated ideas and processes. It's true that in working with HomeKit (and with IoT in general), you're constantly switching from one device to another and one technology to another, but as long as you keep your mind on the principles in these first three chapters, it should stay a unified and coherent whole.

Moving Beyond Talking Refrigerators

"Connect your refrigerator to the Internet, and it will let you know when you're running out of milk!" In June 2000, LG introduced the Internet Digital DIOS refrigerator that promised to fill this need in the world of consumer appliances.

As has been demonstrated over the years, the launch of a major new iPhone or other device from Apple draws crowds of people who sometimes camp out hours or even days before the Apple Store opens. The Internet Digital DIOS refrigerator didn't draw crowds of that size or enthusiasm. In fact, the $20,000 Internet refrigerator did not succeed in the marketplace. (iPhone is a different story.)

It is interesting to compare iPhones and Internet refrigerators. In their first incarnations, they both could be seen as demonstrations of what could be done with new technologies. In that perspective, the products are pretty similar. From another point of view, they were very different. Internet refrigerators promised to put those new technologies to use to do tasks that were familiar to people (e.g., checking to see how much milk is left on the shelf). iPhone used those new technologies to do tasks that hadn't yet been invented. In fact, many of the tasks that are part and parcel of iPhone today weren't even invented by Apple: they've been invented and discovered by people using the technologies and iPhone.

Now it's time to look at what's here in the present with HomeKit (and related Apple automation initiatives). The rest of this chapter brings you up to speed on the technology of HomeKit and what's behind it.

How It Works—The View from the Mountaintop

"Connecting a refrigerator to the Internet" conjures up various images and possibilities, but, as many consumers have realized, when you start thinking about why you would do that and how it would work, things are a little murky.

This section is an overview of the connection process. You'll see that connecting something to the Internet and HomeKit is a bit different from connecting a computer to the Internet. What's important to note is that this is an overall view of most home automation. The details of HomeKit are specific to Apple's approach to home automation, but the overall architecture is not unique.

Remember that this is the high-level view. In other chapters, you'll delve more deeply into the details that make all of the HomeKit environment work together, and you'll see what you can do to make HomeKit and your appliances do exactly what you want.

Introducing Accessories

What exactly is it that you connect to the Internet and HomeKit? As of this writing, it can be a light switch, a thermostat (such as the compatible ones from Ecobee), an electrical plug (the iHome Control Smart Plug is one and iDevices Switch is another), sensors that can check the weather or the status of doors and windows (Elgato makes several), or a hub such as Insteon Hub pro or one of the Lutron bridges.

Before we move on, we need to know how to refer to these in general. You can call them "devices," of course, or even "things" (as in Internet of Things). For this book's discussion of HomeKit, we'll refer to them as *accessories*, which is the term that Apple uses. There are some other HomeKit terms that matter, but they require no special introduction (words like *home* and *room* are used in the everyday senses).

HomeKit Hubs

Now that we know what to call these things (accessories), it's time to move on to see how they can be integrated into HomeKit. Within the home, you have at least one hub. A hub can be an iPad or an Apple TV. It should remain in the home and be powered on at all times. The hub can communicate over the Internet so that remote users can get to it and manage the HomeKit home. If there is more than one hub in the home, they can communicate with one another as well as with the Internet.

Within the home, an accessory communicates using Bluetooth LE (low energy) or the WiFi network. Hubs are often referred to as remote access devices in HomeKit documentation.

> **Tip** See "Setting Up Hubs" in Chapter 9, "Working with iCloud and Users with HomeKit" to see how to set up an Apple TV or iPad as a HomeKit hub that never sleeps. The display can sleep, but the device and its network connection needs to always be available to HomeKit. If you have a TV connected to your Apple TV, it can go to sleep or even be powered off: It is the Apple TV device itself that must remain awake and reachable.

The Basic HomeKit Home

The most basic HomeKit home consists of a hub (typically an Apple TV) and one accessory (perhaps a HomeKit-compatible switch with a lamp plugged into it or a lamp plugged into the wall socket but with a HomeKit-enabled bulb in it). You also need an iOS device (iPhone, iPad, or iPod Touch) to configure your home.

> **Tip** Your accessory (e.g., your lamp), needs to be turned on in the old-fashioned way with its switch. Once it is turned on, you can use HomeKit to adjust it or turn it off, but, particularly with light bulbs, make certain that you've got them powered on before you use HomeKit to adjust them.

Extending HomeKit

There are several basic ways to move beyond the bare-bones HomeKit:

- You can add Accessory, Home, Room, and Scene HomeKit objects

- You can add more HomeKit hub devices—such as another iPad, but start small to get one hub and one device working.

- Bridges: some home automation products such as Philips Hue bulbs require an intermediate connection to their own bridge. The bulb or other device is connected to the bridge and it communicates with its own protocols. The bridge is connected to HomeKit using a HomeKit protocol. Devices such as Hue bulbs are controlled by HomeKit through the bridge, but they do not communicate directly with HomeKit. You don't have to worry about this once it's set up because when you work with HomeKit, you see Hue bulbs just as you see other bulbs: you no longer worry about the bridge (as long as it remains plugged in!).

Summary

The basic architecture of HomeKit focuses on hardware—the iOS devices you use to control HomeKit as well as the accessories such as lamps, door locks, motion sensors, and window shades. There's another side to HomeKit: the software.

You don't need to be a software engineer to know how to put a HomeKit installation together. You need a basic understanding of your accessories and what they can do, but that is probably knowledge that you already have. (Remember, we're talking about light bulbs and lamps, door locks, and other devices that have been around for decades (centuries in the case of door locks).

Perhaps the most important thing to remember about HomeKit software is that users never interact with HomeKit itself (the exception to this is to reset all of HomeKit). Users use apps that typically are designed to work with a single accessory or group of accessories from the same source. In addition to the accessory-specific information, users see HomeKit information (rooms, homes, and scenes). They expect to be able set up a home as well as users; they also need to be able to set up scenes that combine a number of accessories.

Each HomeKit appliance app thus provides an entry into the overall HomeKit environment. With this high-level view of the HomeKit architecture, it's time to focus on specifics.

Chapter 2

Exploring the HomeKit World

Starting with iOS 10 (released in the fall of 2016), HomeKit has an app for users to use to control their HomeKit world. Over the years since its announcement in 2014, Apple has been building out the HomeKit infrastructure—the application program interfaces (APIs) that developers use, the terminology that is shared among HomeKit developers and users (homes, rooms, scenes, and appliances), the third-party HomeKit-enabled products, and, most important, the ideas of how HomeKit can fit into the real world with real people in it. These various tracks (API, third-party products, terminology, and awareness) come together in the Home app.

After you have iOS 10 installed (either by buying a new device equipped with it or downloading it from the App Store), you'll find it on your Home screen as shown in Figure 2-1.

© Jesse Feiler 2016
J. Feiler, *Learn Apple HomeKit on iOS*, DOI 10.1007/978-1-4842-1527-2_2

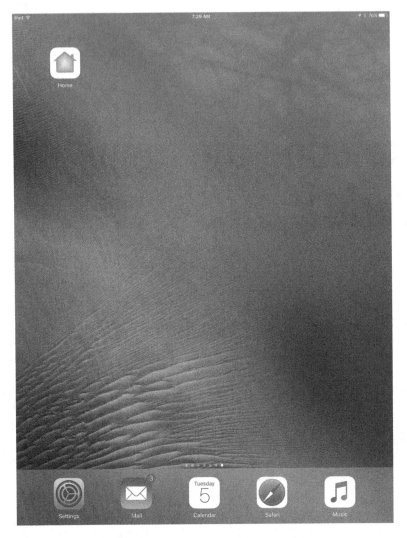

Figure 2-1. Home app on the Home screen

As you'll see in this chapter, with the Home app, you're on your way.

Configuring Your HomeKit Environment

Home provides you with the centralized controls for HomeKit—your home, its rooms, and your accessories (devices like garage doors and lights). Your home as well as all of your accessories are controlled from one or more centralized devices that are always connected to power and to the Internet. Those devices are called *Home Hubs*. One of them is often an Apple TV; you can also use an iPad that is available in your house. Whichever device you use (or both if you use both), HomeKit makes two assumptions.

The first assumption is that the Apple TV or iPad is always powered on and is awake (you'll see how to keep your Apple TV awake with the settings shown at the end of this chapter). Typically, that's from a direct connection to power (an outlet in lay parlance). In the case of an iPad, it can be the battery. In the cases of both Apple TV and iPad, you may be running on battery power that the device itself doesn't know about. This is the case, for example, if you have your own power backup system that kicks in when power from the grid isn't available. These backup devices (usually generators or battery-powered) are becoming more widely available and their prices are coming down. The devices that are plugged in to them, often have no way of knowing if the power is coming from the grid (through a wall outlet) or from the generator or backup system.

No matter your details, HomeKit assumes always-on power so that timers can run all the time.

The second assumption is that your Apple TV and/or iPad will always have an Internet connection. There is some link between power and Internet—if your power goes down, your Internet connection may also be lost.

It's wise to have automatic precautions for your power and Internet to continue functioning in the case of outages, and modern devices rely on that happening—that is, they rely on your environment providing whatever contingency planning is necessary to having continuous power and Internet.

Now it's on to more specific requirements for HomeKit.

Starting from an Apple ID

You need an Apple ID for Home. An Apple ID uniquely identifies you, and it is normally linked to a valid credit card. (You can work around the credit card link in some cases—see https://appleid.apple.com/us for more details. (Note that the URL (uniform resource locator) provided here is for the United States. Log on to apple.com in your home country and search on Apple ID to find your localized information.)

When you create your Home in Home, it's yours—that is, it is identified with your Apple ID. Within Home, you can create multiple homes, rooms, and accessories, but they're all part of your home that's linked to your Apple ID.

Many people have more than one Apple ID. Sometimes it happens by accident over time, particularly as Apple ID has evolved. Other times it's deliberate, as is the case for developers and authors who must have separate Apple IDs for the accounts they use to manage their apps and their iBooks.

You can use Family Sharing to share a single Apple ID among several other family members, each of whom has an Apple ID. Family Sharing is designed largely for kids so that the single organizer (an adult who's a parent or guardian) gets the bill for everyone. This allows kids under 13 to have their own Apple IDs and to purchase—with permission—from the family account.

You have at least one Apple ID already if you have bought anything from iTunes or the App stores. In almost all cases, it's best to use an existing Apple ID for Home. If you start creating new Apple IDs for each use, you may wind up with a bit of a mess.

Once you have your Apple ID and Home installed on your Apple TV or an iPad, you're ready to go.

Quick Start with iPad

If you want to jump right in, here's how you can get started with Home on iPad. Once you've installed iOS 10 (or purchased an iPad with it preloaded), just tap Home as shown previously in Figure 2-1.

> **Caution**   This is what you see the first time. If you've ever launched Home before, you won't see these steps: Don't worry! Everything that's shown here and that matters is also described in the section "Managing Home Settings."

After you've tapped Home for the first time, here's what you see and what you do:

1. The screen shown in Figure 2-2 is your first-time introduction. All you have to do is tap Get Started.

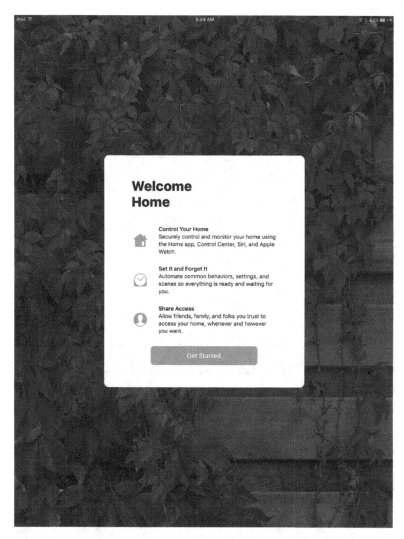

Figure 2-2. Get started

2. The first time you use Home, you'll be prompted
    to allow access to location while the app is in use,
    as shown in Figure 2-3. You can use some parts of
    HomeKit without using Location Services, but many
    features rely on your location, so you'll severely limit
    its usability if you tap Don't Allow. So do tap Allow.
    (See the Tip later on how to reset this.)

Figure 2-3. Allow access to location

3. Once you've managed Location Services, you're in as shown in Figure 2-4.

Figure 2-4. Start to use Home

You can explore Home at this point, but if you can resist the temptation to jump right in, Chapter 3 will take you on a guided tour. Here's one preview to whet your appetite (and it will help you navigate in Home). At the bottom of the screen shown in Figure 2-4, note the tab bar with two tabs: Home and Automation. Tap Automation to get a preview of what's in store as shown in Figure 2-5.

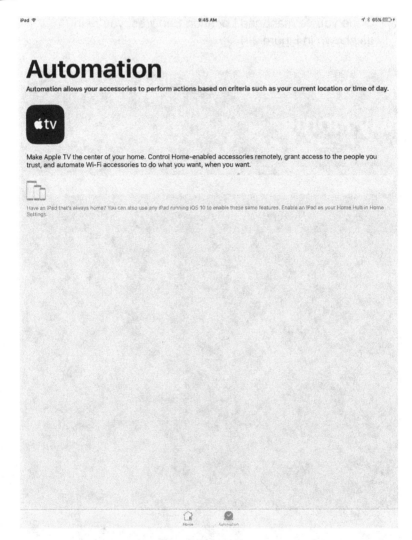

Figure 2-5. Get a preview of automation in Home

You can always switch from one area of Home to another using the tab bar at the bottom.

Managing Home Settings

As with most iOS apps, you can manage settings for your apps using Settings from the Home screen. Some settings are set here, and others are set inside the app itself. Settings typically manages the most general settings as well as settings that can (sometimes must) be set outside the app.

> **Tip** An example of in-app settings compared to Settings app settings is often iCloud use. When you first run an iCloud-enabled app, you are typically asked if you want to use iCloud. If you later want to change that decision, you make the decision in Settings rather than in the app. This structure enables the app to make the necessary internal adjustments when you turn iCloud on or off for the app. Doing it in this way means that the actual work of switching to or from iCloud can be done behind the scenes rather than inside the app. It also means that you can make the change to or from iCloud when the app isn't even running.

1. On your iPad, tap Settings and select Home from the list of built-in apps as shown in Figure 2-6.

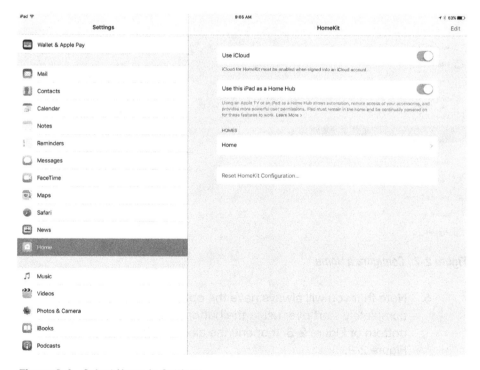

Figure 2-6. Select Home in Settings

You will probably want to use iCloud for HomeKit at some time in the future, so you might as well turn it on here. Remember, that you need an Apple ID for iCloud. That should be the same Apple ID you're using with HomeKit.

2. You also can use this opportunity to designate the device you're using (an iPad or Apple TV) as Home Hub, remember you can have more than one.

3. You start with a single Home as you see in Figure 2-6.

4. You can tap the disclosure triangle to configure it further as shown in Figure 2-7.

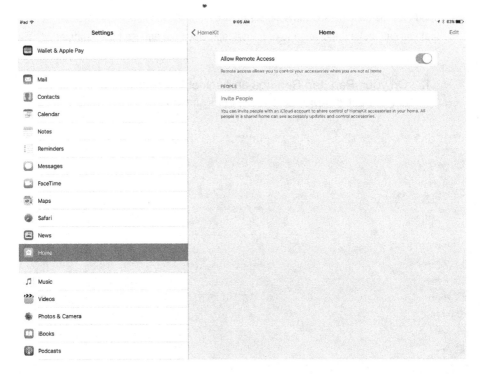

Figure 2-7. Configure a Home

5. Note that you will always have the option to completely start over using the button shown at the bottom of Figure 2-6. It opens the alert shown in Figure 2-8.

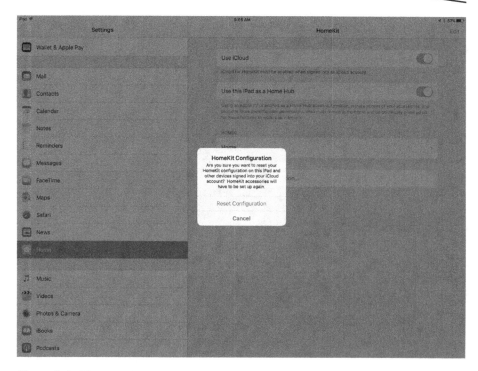

Figure 2-8. *You can always reset Home*

> **Caution**   This is the way to reset Home. You can achieve a similar result by removing Home from your device. As is the case with removing any app, you'll remove its data. That is a brute-force way of resetting Home, and it is definitely not recommended.

Moving into Your Home

When you launch Home after configuring Settings (if you do that now—remember it's optional) you may see the basic screen shown in Figure 2-9.

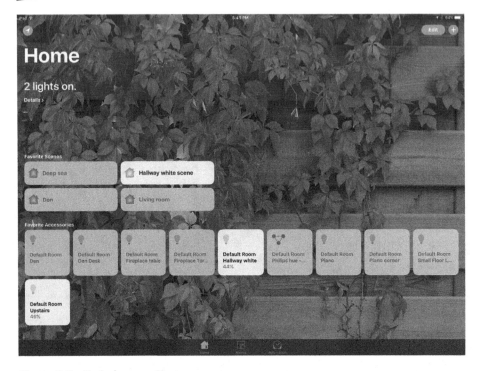

Figure 2-9. Exploring your Home

This is your Home as shown in the app. What you see will vary depending on your specific home, its rooms, and its appliances. You can configure the background image as well as just about everything in the view. The background image can be a photo of your home. Maybe you'd like the background image to be the view you see from the bedroom window.

Tip   Remember, Home (the app) can manage several homes, so the background image that you choose for a specific home should very clearly remind you what it is. For a dorm room at school (yes, a single room can be a Home in some cases), you might choose a photo of a campus landmark. For your actual home (i.e., "the place where, when you have to go there, they have to take you in," as Robert Frost wrote), you might choose a photo of the backyard. Why would you make these photo choices? If your Home image shows your bed and desk covered with computer, papers, lunch (date of lunch undetermined), and so forth, you may not be able to quickly notice which of those photos is which place.

Add and Configure a Home

You can see the default Home, and you may have explored it. Now it's time to build your own. To add a new Home, tap the arrow in the top left of the window shown previously in Figure 2-9.

You'll see the Add Home alert as shown in Figure 2-10.

Figure 2-10. Add a Home

As you see in Figure 2-10, you can name your Home. You'll be able to invite people to control the Home accessories (that will be discussed in Chapter 3). You can take a photo for your Home wallpaper or choose from an existing image. You can come back here later on to rename the Home, change the wallpaper, or invite people to control the accessories.

Edit or Add a Room

Use the Rooms tab in the tab bar at the bottom of a Home window to look at your Rooms. Use the list icon at the top left of the window to see the options for Rooms as shown in Figure 2-11. You can configure the Room you're looking at or add a new Room.

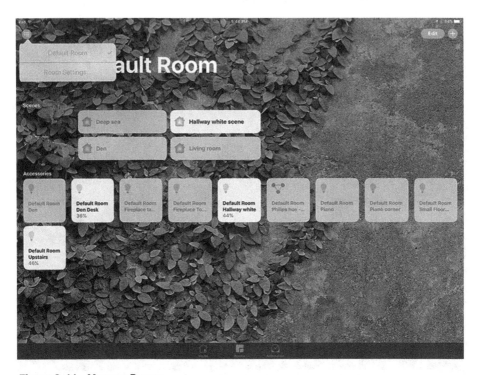

Figure 2-11. Manage Rooms

If you choose Room Settings, you'll see the alert shown in Figure 2-12 where you can add a new Room or configure an existing Room.

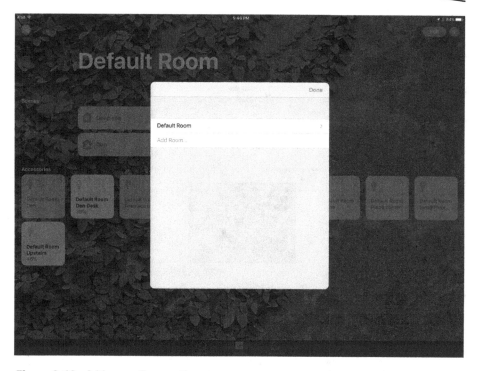

Figure 2-12. Add or configure a Room

Remember that the default room is named Default Room. Use the disclosure triangle to the right of its name to rename it (or any room). When you tap the disclosure triangle, you can set the room data as shown in Figure 2-13.

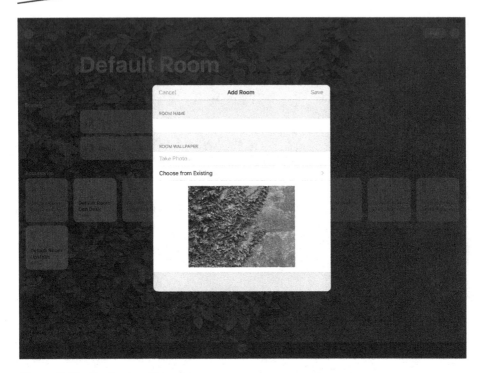

Figure 2-13. Configure a Room

Notice the pattern here: set the name for a Home, Room, or (in the following section) accessory. Set its wallpaper from an existing image or take a photo. That's the routine: name, wallpaper, Done (top right) or Cancel (top left).

Add and Configure an Accessory

Accessories are lamps, garage doors, or any of devices that will be known to HomeKit and controlled by it. Add an accessory from the + at the top right of a Home or a Room (switch between them with the tab bar at the bottom of the screen. Figure 2-14 shows adding an accessory to a Home.

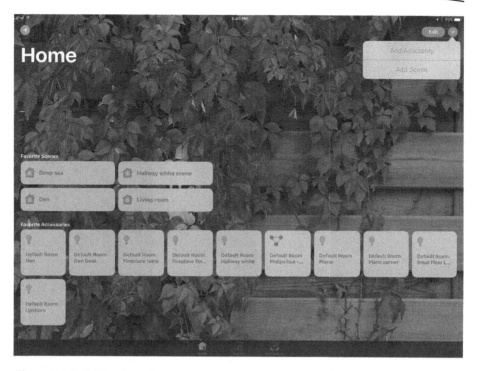

Figure 2-14. Add and configure an accessory

> **Note** *Scenes* are combinations of accessories and schedules. They're what
> you use to pull the pieces of Home automation together. They're discussed in
> Chapter 3.

Adding an accessory starts the process by which HomeKit searches for
the accessory and configures it for HomeKit. Figure 2-15 shows the initial
screen, and Chapter 3 describes the steps.

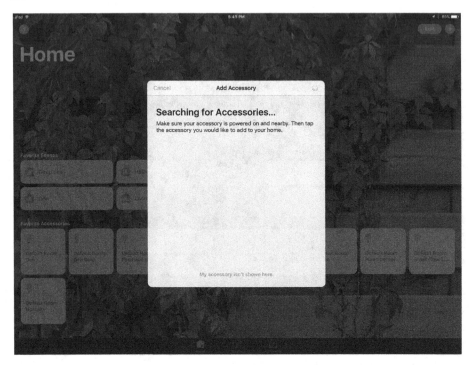

Figure 2-15. Start to configure an accessory

Adding Scenes— The Practical Part of HomeKit

In Chapter 2, you see the very logical and recognizable structure of HomeKit homes: the home contains rooms, and each room contains accessories such as lamps, sensors for smoke or temperature, and a whole variety of devices such as garage door openers (well, maybe not *inside* a room) and automated window blinds. You can use HomeKit to manage all the rooms and accessories by turning them on and off or adjusting their settings. You can also use HomeKit to check the settings of accessories, such as whether they're on or off as well as their brightness and color (in the case of bulbs).

This is a nice structure, and it's quite recognizable. As you proceed through the book, you're going to see how to control these things, and when you get a bit further into the book, you'll find out how to automate them.

In many ways, this pattern (home ➤ room ➤ accessory) is what you live with. Watch how you turn your accessories on and off during your day at home. For many people, the turning on and off depends on the time of day, where you are in the home, and what you are doing. When you go into a small room (particularly at night), you turn on the light, and that light is often a ceiling fixture. A larger room may have a single ceiling fixture, but, in many rooms there are several lamps and perhaps not even one ceiling fixture. There may be a reading/working light on the desk, and a floor lamp by an easy chair, and perhaps a small nightlight you turn on overnight to prevent people (including yourself) from walking into furniture.

© Jesse Feiler 2016
J. Feiler, *Learn Apple HomeKit on iOS*, DOI 10.1007/978-1-4842-1527-2_3

Many people organize these lights into groups so that a single light switch turns on several of them at the same time. It's not particularly burdensome to walk into your living room in the evening and turn on three separate lights, but it's not necessary with various mechanical devices (e.g., power strips).

What Is a Scene?

HomeKit *scenes* are just a digital version of the multiple-light scenario. A scene is a set of accessories each of which can be added to the scene with its own specific settings.

Creating Basic Scenes

You can create a scene for evening in your living room that turns on the floor lamp by a sofa as well as a reading lamp on the desk. Because accessories can be more than lamps, the evening scene could also include a window shade accessory. When the scene is constructed from the accessories, you can set their attributes so that in the scenario just described, the scene could be formally defined as follows:

- Floor lamp: soft white (2550 K), 50% brightness
- Reading lamp: standard white (2400 K), 80% brightness
- Window shade: closed

COLOR TEMPERATURE

Color temperature (measured on the Kelvin scale and abbreviated K) is the description of the type of light emitted by a bulb or other light source. (It's actually more complex than this— you can find an excellent reference on Wikipedia at https://en.wikipedia.org/w/index.php?title=Color_temperature&oldid=740585423. Without getting too deep into the details, consider these K values and what they represent (the representations are subjective and not part of a formal classification):

- 1850 K candle flame
- 2400 K standard incandescent light bulb
- 2550 K soft white incandescent light bulb
- 3000 K warm white compact fluorescent bulbs
- 6500 K overcast daylight
- 15,000-27,000 K clear blue sky

Another scene can be created to end the evening. A go-to-bed scene might look like this:

- Floor lamp: soft white (2550 K), 10% brightness

- Reading lamp: standard bulb (2400 K), 0% brightness

- Window shade: closed

Scenes Can Involve Several Rooms

Think back to the home ➤ room ➤ accessory pattern, and you can see that this all fits very well. But now you can modify this scene in a way that breaks that pattern. Consider the following variation on the evening scene:

- Floor lamp: soft white (2550 K), 50% brightness

- Reading lamp: standard bulb (2400 K), 80% brightness

- Window shade: closed

- **Bedside lamp: soft white (2550 K), 75% brightness**

What is broken in the home ➤ room ➤ accessory pattern is that now the go-to-bed scene includes a lamp in another room (the bedside lamp in the bedroom). This is important whether you use scenes manually from an iOS device or as part of an automation. The collection of accessories in a scene doesn't rely on the rooms those accessories are in. If you move the accessories from one room to another, the scene will still function. (You may be surprised at the results until you realize that the lamp on the coffee table used to be on the bedside table.)

Scenes Can Be Automated and Respond to Siri

Another important aspect of scenes is that each scene has a name, and Siri recognizes those names. Thus, scenes are critically important for automation (described in the final chapter of the book) as well as for Siri. If you want to move beyond building a complex replacement for a light switch that costs less than a dollar, having automation and voice recognition tools is key.

Scenes Are Instantaneous

There's one final aspect of scenes to consider: they are instantaneous. This doesn't mean that they are activated immediately when you tap a scene button or get to the time a trigger is set to function: it takes time for messages to be sent over the network. Rather, it's important to note that a scene describes accessories and their settings at a single point in time. If you manually turn a light that is part of a scene on or off, it will remain on or off until the next scene that involves it is activated. A by-product of this is the fact that if you want lights to be on for a period of time (or a door to be locked or unlocked for a period of time), you will need two scenes: one to turn it on/lock it and another to turn it off/unlock it.

Because each scene is independent, if you construct a scene to turn on several lights, you must construct another scene (or use Siri or iPad controls) to turn off the lights.

Working with Scenes

To start working with scenes, take a look at your home screen in the Home app as shown in Figure 3-1.

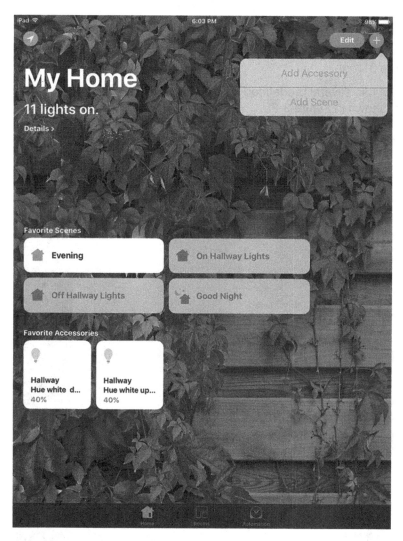

Figure 3-1. See scenes on the home screen

This screen provides a summary of your home. Your favorite scenes are shown here. This is an excellent place to put scenes that involve several rooms: you just mark them as favorites.

Creating a Scene

From the home screen, use the + in the top right to add a scene as you see in Figure 3-1.

HomeKit has several predefined scenes, as you will see after you tap Add Scene (shown in Figure 3-2).

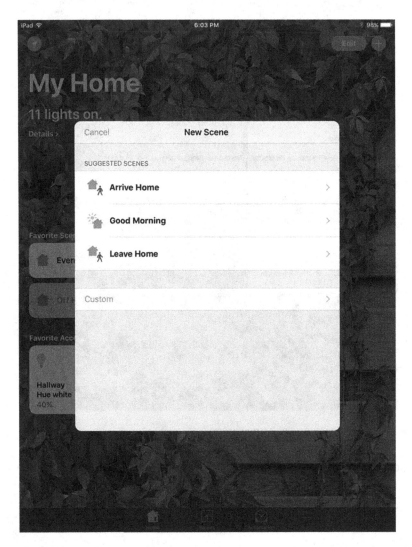

Figure 3-2. Create a new scene

These scenes have names that should get you started thinking. They are not predefined beyond their names because they have to use your accessories.

You can create your own scene by tapping Custom. If you create a custom scene, you can name it as in the alert shown in Figure 3-3.

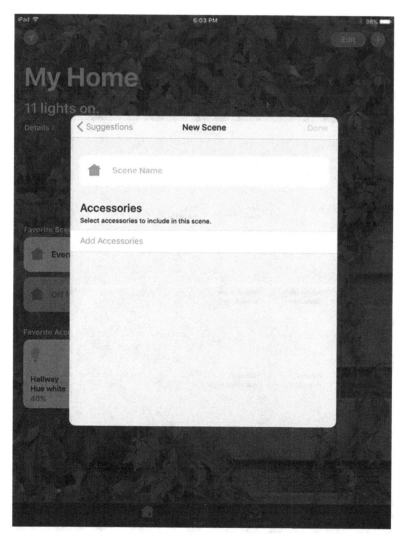

Figure 3-3. Name a scene

Adding Accessories

After you name a scene, you can add accessories to it as you see in
Figure 3-4. (You can always come back later to rename it and add or remove
accessories.)

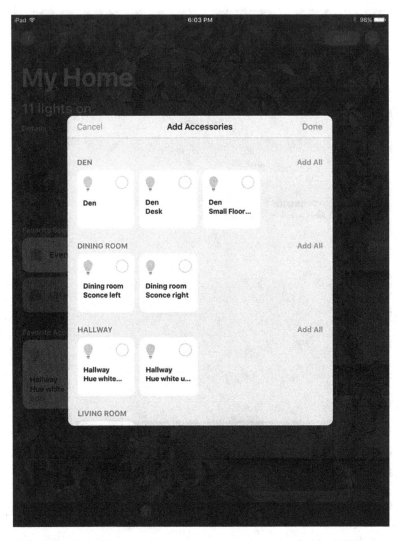

Figure 3-4. Add accessories

You'll see your rooms and their accessories as shown in Figure 3-4. You can add any accessory by tapping the circle at the top right. You can also add all the accessories in a room by tapping Add All. Figure 3-5 shows all of the accessories added in that way for the dining room. Note that Add All for the dining room is now changed to Remove All.

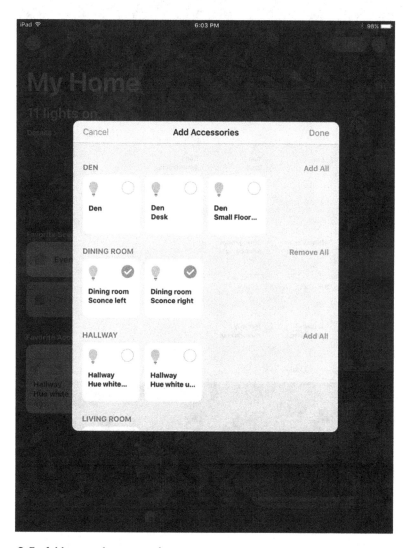

Figure 3-5. Add a room's accessories

As you see in Figure 3-6, you can also add or remove individual accessories in a room just by tapping that round circle in the top right of the accessory.

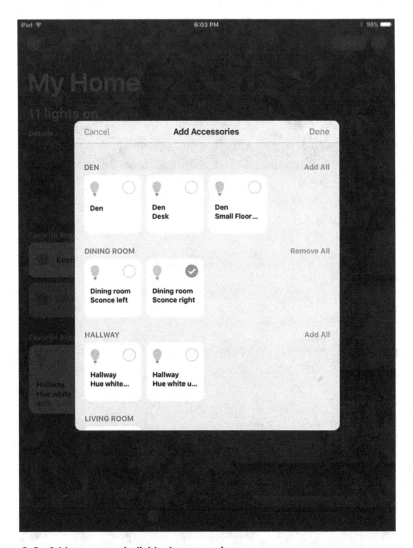

Figure 3-6. Add or remove individual accessories

Tap Done at the top right to finish adding or removing accessories.

Adjusting Accessories

When you tap Done, you're back to the basic scene description as shown in Figure 3-7. You can rename it here, but what's important is that you can now adjust your accessories and test the scene.

> **Tip**   At least while you're testing, add the scene to Favorites on the home page as you can see in Figure 3-7.

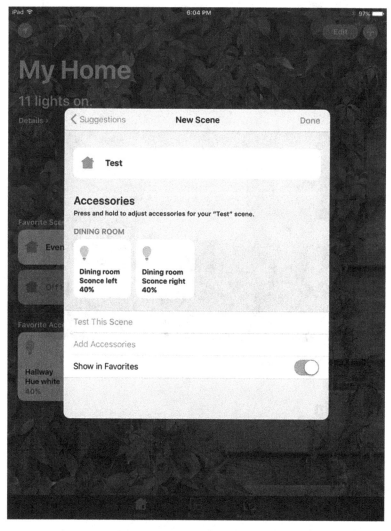

Figure 3-7. Adjust your scene and accessories

To adjust an accessory, tap and hold it to open the detail view shown in Figure 3-8. Remember that this view will be different depending on the type of accessory you are dealing with. Figure 3-8 shows a light bulb detail view. You can slide the divider on the bulb up or down to adjust the brightness.

Figure 3-8. Adjust an accessory

Finishing Up

When you're finished, you can see your new scene on the home screen (at least you can if you added it as a favorite as shown in Figure 3-7). Figure 3-9 shows the home screen now.

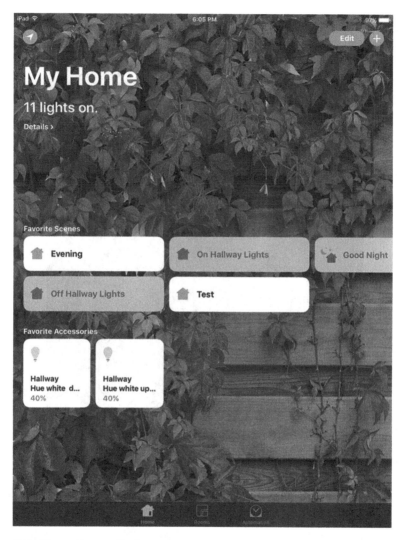

Figure 3-9. *New scene on the home screen*

Editing Your Scene

Tap and hold a scene on the home screen (or on a room screen—the room screen shows all scenes for that room). When you lift your finger after the hold, you'll see the scene as shown in Figure 3-10. Tap Details at the bottom of the screen to edit it.

Figure 3-10. Start to edit the scene

As you see in Figure 3-11, you're back to being able to edit the scene. If you made it a favorite just for testing, you can turn that off here.

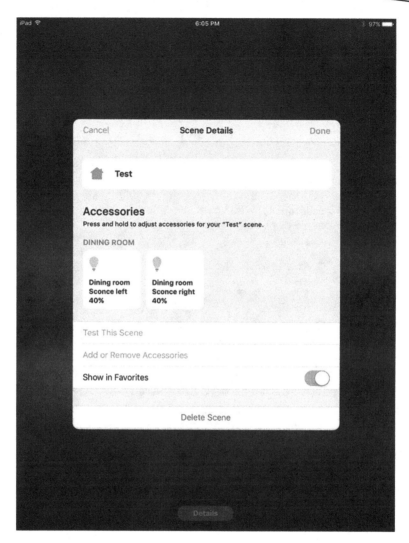

Figure 3-11. Edit the scene

You can delete a scene from here as well. If you do, you'll need to confirm it as you see in Figure 3-12.

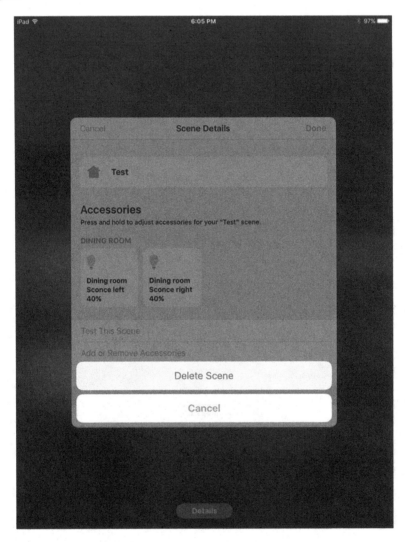

Figure 3-12. Delete a scene

It's important to remember that scenes build on the accessories in your home, but they do not modify those accessories. This means that you can delete a scene without disturbing anything else. (If the scene is used in an automation, you will upset the automation, of course, but you won't affect the accessories themselves.)

Chapter 4

Exploring Your Development Environment

For almost every HomeKit developer, getting started means setting up a new environment and, in some cases, a new way of working. If you're a developer who's familiar with iOS, you're well on your way to HomeKit . . . as long as your familiarity includes the most recent version or two of iOS. Lots of things have changed in the decade (barely) since iOS emerged from iPhone OS (which in turn only emerged from NeXTSTEP and OpenStep after Apple bought NeXT in 1997).

As a HomeKit developer, you need to become familiar with HomeKit itself in addition to iOS. And just to keep you on your toes, you'll need to start using the latest version of Xcode, the integrated development environment (IDE) for iOS and Mac apps.

You may need to explore a new programming language (Swift), and, perhaps, you'll need to become familiar with event-driven programming. This may seem like a tall order, but, in fact, these are common aspects of today's development environments, and whether you're developing for HomeKit or another modern API (application program interface) (even one on other platforms), you'll probably need to know at least some of these things.

So let's get started.

© Jesse Feiler 2016
J. Feiler, *Learn Apple HomeKit on iOS*, DOI 10.1007/978-1-4842-1527-2_4

Getting Developer Access

Apple is making it increasingly easy for developers—including those new to the platforms—to develop apps for macOS and iOS. If you're already an Apple developer, you have your developer credentials and can skip this section and move on to "Downloading the Tools." If you've never been an Apple developer, this section provides you with an overview. And if you've been an Apple developer but haven't used your account for a while (since about 2015), there have been a number of changes (simplifications) that you'll need to know about.

What has not changed is that you need an Apple ID to access the full range of developer tools. An Apple ID is free for the asking as long as you are over 13 (the age may vary by the country you are in) and have a valid e-mail address (to be used to confirm your identity). Your Apple ID can be used for purchases in iTunes, the App Store, and the Mac App Store. If you already have one, you can use it as a developer.

However, note that as a developer, you may want to have a separate Apple ID account. In fact, if you are an iBooks Author, at least at the moment, the Apple ID you use to publish in the iBooks Store needs to be separate from your developer Apple ID. (Check out developer.apple.com for the latest information for your country.)

What is most important is that you need an Apple ID (free) and that Apple ID gives you access to development tools like Xcode (the IDE) and the iOS Simulator that you can use to test your iOS apps.

With your free Apple ID, you can build apps and test them on your own devices. (This capability is new beginning with Xcode 7 in 2015. Before that, you had to be part of a developer program.)

Speaking of which, you may want to become a member of one of Apple's developer programs at some time. Although you can now install your apps on your own devices without being a developer program member, you cannot submit them to an App Store without being a registered developer. This means that you cannot distribute them to other people. In order to have access to the App Store, you need to join one of the developer programs at developer.apple.com. There are several types of programs, but most developers opt for the $99/year basic membership that gives you access to the App Store.

> **Note**   Your developer program membership typically includes two Developer Technical Support incidents (DTIs) a year. You can buy more of them at $99 for two. A DTI allows you to ask a question of an Apple engineer. It can be broad, such as "where do I find information about . . .," but most developers use the more detailed technical support. You can submit an app (or part of an app) with which you're having trouble as a developer. (DTIs don't cover support for using other people's apps, but they do cover support for using Xcode.) An Apple engineer will review your code and help you pinpoint problems and solutions. This is an incredibly valuable resource, particularly if you are an independent developer who can't turn to a colleague to help you out (and you'll of course offer to return the favor some time).

With your Apple ID (whether for your personal use or a separate one to use as a developer), you're ready to download and install the tools to start building HomeKit apps.

Reviewing the Tools

Membership in one of the Apple developer programs, as described in the previous section, gives you access to the tools you need. You don't need all of them to start, but here is a review of what they are and what you need to look for.

Don't be put off by this list: it's designed to give you an idea of what is involved. The standard download of Xcode includes all the current versions of these tools. Options in Xcode let you automatically receive updates as they are released. (You can also receive updates only on demand. Typically, automatic updates are for minor—"dot"—releases such as 8.3.1, as opposed to major releases such as 8 or even 8.3.)

Furthermore, remember that Xcode and these tools are available without charge. Some of the development features may require a developer program membership, but the basic development tools and the tools to deploy them on your own devices are free.

> **Tip**   The full download may take a while. You may want to go to the Energy Saver panel in System Preferences to prevent automatic sleep until the download is complete. You also may choose to do the full download at a time when your system and communications environments are not being stressed— overnight is a good choice in many cases.

The tools fall into several interrelated categories.

- Languages
- Frameworks
- Simulators

Languages: Swift and Objective-C

Before Apple bought NeXT and launched OS X (and later, iOS), developers used a variety of programming languages. The original Mac was based on Pascal, and the operating system contained a bit of low-level code as well. Over time, the operating system also included some C and C++. The NeXT acquisition brought with it the Objective-C programming language which had been developed along with NeXT (you can find more about the history on Wikipedia which has several excellent articles on it).

Objective-C remained the primary language for Mac and iOS for a long time, and it still is a major language both for the operating system and for application programming. However, as with other object-oriented programming languages, advances in hardware and software opened up new opportunities. Objective-C remained (and to this day still remains) primarily under Apple's management. In 2014, Apple released the first version of a new programming language: Swift. It takes advantage of many advances in operating system and software development technologies. Swift is now an open source project, and there are versions available on Linux and the IBM Swift Sandbox web site (https://swiftlang.ng.bluemix. net/?cm_mmc=developerWorks-_-dWdevcenter-_-swift-_-lp&cm_mc_ uid=5857313470051460291775l&cm_mc_sid_50200000=1460291775#/repl)

> **Note**   Both Objective-C and Swift remain widely used on Apple products and on third-party apps. Although Apple's demonstrations and example code typically use Swift today, Apple often provides alternate versions in Objective-C. Furthermore, considering the enormous amount of legacy software, both languages will continue in use for the foreseeable future.

If you are new to development on Apple platforms, Swift is generally the easiest language to learn; you'll eventually need a simple understanding of Objective-C in some special cases (this is akin to the distinction between passive—reading—knowledge of a natural language and active—speaking or writing—knowledge of a natural language).

Frameworks

Frameworks have evolved over the years. Today, the term refers to a collection of reusable libraries just as it has done for many years. Those libraries can also contain resources such as images and strings. What you may not have noticed is the scope of frameworks. In the world of Apple's software, most of today's frameworks can be traced back to NeXTSTEP. Two major frameworks and sets of frameworks emerged: core frameworks and higher-level frameworks focusing on the user interface (this is a vast simplification, but it is sufficient to provide a background for your HomeKit development).

Over the years, smaller frameworks have been created as part of the operating systems. Their names make it clear what they are. At the core level, there are frameworks such as CoreLocation, CoreGraphics, CoreText, CoreVideo, and more. At the interface level, there are frameworks such as AddressBook, CloudKit, UIKit (for views and controls), Security framework, WebKit, and the like.

Frameworks are packaged to be reusable. When you first create a project in Xcode, you choose the type of project to create and the relevant frameworks are automatically installed in it. You can add others as you go along. (Don't worry about discarding frameworks you don't use: the Xcode build process doesn't copy unused frameworks into your runnable code.)

A key feature of frameworks is that they can be versioned. This means that they can be developed and revised in parallel with the code that uses the frameworks, but the connection is fairly loose because you can have multiple versions of a framework in your development environment at the same time.

Frameworks have most recently evolved to allow the sharing of code across Apple platforms. If you have an API that you create to manage your data, you may package it (or an interface to it) into a framework that is totally platform-neutral. You can then include the framework in your code for iOS, macOS, watchOS, and tvOS. In each of those environments, you can write the user interface that is appropriate, but the framework itself may be platform-agnostic.

What this means is that you'll be using frameworks that are part of the development kits from Apple, and, most likely, you'll be creating smaller frameworks for your own use. (This latter use of frameworks has become increasingly important over the last few years with the need to write code for both iOS and OS X as well as now for watchOS and tvOS.)

Simulators

It has always been a challenge to write code for products that don't yet exist (early Macintosh application code as well as the operating system was written on the Lisa computer, and, even today, we write code for iOS devices on Macs).

The code for not-yet-existing devices has to be tested somehow, and so we have simulators available to run the code on a host—your Mac in these cases. Today, you can download simulators for various devices and operating systems.

With your standard Xcode download, you'll find the current versions of the operating systems for iOS, macOS, watchOS, and tvOS. You'll also typically get the immediately prior versions automatically. You'll be able to download even earlier versions if you want them. At some times, registered developers are able to download pre-release or developer preview versions of upcoming operating systems. These downloads are covered by nondisclosure agreements that you agree to when you become a registered developer.

In addition to versions of the operating systems, you'll also be able to simulate various devices. The pre-release versions of operating systems are typically available several months before their public release. Pre-release versions of hardware (e.g., new versions of iPad), are typically less widely available until the public announcement.)

The most important thing to remember about simulators is that they are only simulators: nothing can do fully accurate testing except for the actual device. Some features (iCloud synchronization is one) are totally under your control: it doesn't happen automatically as it does on actual devices, but you trigger it with a command on the iOS Simulator. This lets you manage your testing.

Simulating HomeKit Accessories

HomeKit introduces a whole new set of devices to simulate: the third-party HomeKit accessories. These present a difficult task both for Apple and for developers because the development of these third-party products is under the control of the third parties.

Apple has created a tool that lets you simulate these accessories whether they exist yet or not. That tool itself (HomeKit Catalog) is available for your use. Its source code is downloadable from developer.apple.com and is discussed in Chapter 5. If you want to get a jump, you can download the HomeKit Accessory Simulator from `https://developer.apple.com/library/content/documentation/NetworkingInternet/Conceptual/HomeKitDeveloperGuide/EnablingHomeKit/EnablingHomeKit.html#//apple_ref/doc/uid/TP40015050-CH2-SW3`.

Getting Set Up

You can download the current version of Xcode from the Mac App Store or from the Xcode page on the Developer site: https://developer.apple.com/xcode/. If you go to developer.apple.com and register as a developer, you can follow the links there. Downloads from the developer site may give you more information than just the Mac App Store download, particularly if you have registered for one of the development programs.

What's Next

Download the current version of Xcode (or update your older version). Try to build some of the built-in projects to get a feel for the process.

Next, it's time to move on. Start by getting a variety of HomeKit accessories that you can use for testing. Put your wallet away! Chapter 5 helps you build your own HomeKit accessories to use for simulating your HomeKit app. Before you know it, you'll have HomeKit lights, locks, sensors, and garage door openers in your (virtual) hands.

Working with HomeKit Accessories

In the previous chapters you've seen the basis of HomeKit and its architecture. Now it's time to put it to work, and that involves accessories—your lights, door openers and lock mechanisms, sensors, and the whole range of HomeKit-enabled devices that you find in ever-increasing numbers in local stores and on the Internet. (It's like the old saw: if a tree falls in the forest and no one is around to hear it, does it make a sound?) Without accessories to be controlled, HomeKit does nothing. This chapter shows you how to put HomeKit to work.

Set Up a HomeKit Test Lab

You can read this chapter as an overview and then refer to it as necessary. After you've set up a few accessories, you get into the swing of things and it's very easy to add more or to modify the ones that you have installed. If you're antsy to get started right away, one way to dive in is to set up a HomeKit test lab. Don't worry: it's simple and not very expensive. In fact, you may already have everything you need. The HomeKit test lab consists of a small lamp with a HomeKit-compatible bulb. (A bedside lamp is just the right size.) You can also test with a HomeKit-compatible outlet like the iDevices Switch ($49 at the time of this writing from the Apple Store `http://www.apple.com/shop/product/HJDA2LL/A/idevices-switch?fno` `de=7f25f48c45679a233b5f95df8a36e8c57b1a59eec22a1199de38581ece45` `f61e35befe08d1b8717ea467a33ece28d6f31812356449f121305b81329c678-` `02ef1fda2f5ae7635b27545b0c648dfa77050b432ea48991f2da917f39542d5bff8e3)`

© Jesse Feiler 2016
J. Feiler, *Learn Apple HomeKit on iOS*, DOI 10.1007/978-1-4842-1527-2_5

Plug anything you want into the switch and control the switch and the plugged-in device from HomeKit. Both of these test labs let you get to work with HomeKit right away.

Your light bulb or switch should be marked as compatible with HomeKit. (If you're using a switch for a lamp to test with, the switch needs to be HomeKit-compatible, but the bulb in the lamp can be ordinary.) Don't just ask for something that works with a generic home automation product. Look for the logo shown in Figure 5-1.

Figure 5-1. Check for HomeKit compatibility

For an updated list of accessories, look on apple.com. This list varies by country so search for HomeKit on local your version of apple.com. In the United States, the list is at `https://support.apple.com/en-us/HT204903` WARNING (or TIP): Watch for the hub!

In addition to compatibility with HomeKit, when you buy a device, make certain that it does not require an external hub. HomeKit will be your hub, and it will communicate either directly with your accessories over WiFi or it will communicate with a third-party hub that then communicates to the third-party accessory. The iDevices Switch described in this section does not require a hub so you can just plug it in and start. Philips Hue bulbs require the Philips hub (included in many of their starter kits). Some of the cheaper home automation products require external hubs that are not included in the packaging.

Set Up HomeKit

Now that you have your appliance set up (that's the tree in your forest), it's time to control it. You've already seen the basic HomeKit structure, but now is the time to use it for real.

> **Tip**   HomeKit has evolved over several years as Apple and third-party developers have refined the products and brought them to market. The description of HomeKit in this book, and, particularly, in this chapter, reflects HomeKit as it is in iOS 10. iOS 10 is really the first large-scale deployment of HomeKit. It's installed as part of the standard installation on iPad and Apple TV. Also, it incorporates some changes that make it easier to use than previous versions. If you need to check for further information or look at discussions on the web, check the dates of the material carefully. Look for iOS 10 or 2016: material from earlier versions and dates is likely to no longer be correct.

There's a hub to HomeKit: the central location from which everything is controlled. With today's HomeKit, that hub is typically an Apple TV, but it can also be an iPad. Whatever it is, it should be something that is powered on at all times and that has Internet and WiFi connections. In the case of an Apple TV, the TV itself need not be on: in fact, most unused TV screens will conserve energy and power off or sleep while the Apple TV continues to function and draw a small amount of power. If you're using an iPad, it should be plugged in; it, too, will draw a relatively small amount of power when it's simply connected and there is no user interaction.

If your hub (Apple TV or iPad) loses power or runs out of battery power, don't worry. It should pick up right where it left off when power is restored. The only exception is if the power failure occurs while you are adjusting the settings. In that case, you may lose some data, but you can always restore it.

It's not necessary to use an uninterrupted power supply (UPS) with your Apple TV or iPad, but, as with any device other than the most basic, a surge suppressor is a good idea.

As described in Chapters 2 and 3, you can start from the default room in your default home. Before going ahead to set up everything, it's a good idea to resist that temptation and get one lamp or one outlet working.

Tip   If you have a home automation hub like the Philips Hue bridge, your lights, rooms, and scenes, are often described there. Look at the documentation for that product for a guide to integrating it with HomeKit. In the case of the Philips Hue system, you can follow the directions on the Philips web site to add the hub itself as a HomeKit appliance. You add the hub and then use the Hue iOS app to move appliances over. Once HomeKit recognizes them, you can move them into rooms and use them in automations. Now that HomeKit is stable and deployed, these third-party products are often being refined, so check the vendor's web site for guidance. Because HomeKit and third-party hubs have a bit of overlap in their functionality, you may have to do a little bit of fiddling until the dust settles on this integration. Look at the web sites for HomeKit and your hub for further guidance. You may need to be a bit flexible and imaginative. For example, when working with the Hue app and a Philips bridge, you'll soon realize that adding lights to Siri (in the Hue app) means adding them to HomeKit. Once things are set up, it's terrific. You can reset your entire HomeKit environment by going to Settings->Privacy->HomeKit. If you've added a Hue bridge, you'll see it there. Make sure it's turned on in Settings. Also notice the Reset HomeKit configuration button: it doesn't hurt to plan from the start that you'll experiment and then wipe everything out. That's usually better than trying to convert your experimentation to the final HomeKit configuration you want to use.

If you do want to add some accessories, you may wind up with a home that looks like Figure 5-2. Most of these are lamps, but you'll notice a Philips hue bridge in the lower right. Remember that on the HomeKit home screen, these are favorites: the actual data for the favorite items is stored elsewhere.

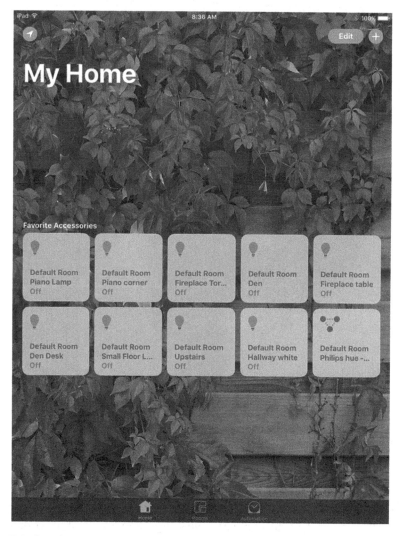

Figure 5-2. Favorite accessories on the home screen

Figure 5-2 shows the default first screen: it's your favorite accessories no matter where in the home they are. (This is the Home button in the bottom toolbar.) You can start to hone in on a specific room with the Rooms button in the bottom toolbar as shown in Figure 5-3.

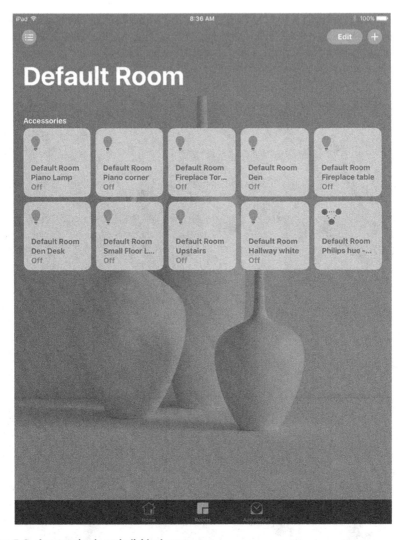

Figure 5-3. Accessories in an individual room

Many people set up HomeKit room by room. You can then copy critical accessories to Favorites so they show up in the Home tab on the bottom toolbar. This is a simple and powerful way of getting HomeKit to work for you, but it's only the very beginning.

Setting Up a Room

Whether you start from the default room that is created for you by default or are creating your own rooms (maybe a tiny room that contains only that test lamp and bulb that you're using for experimentation), you can configure the settings for each room.

To start configuring a room, tap the Rooms button in the bottom toolbar. Use the List button in the top left to show a list of rooms as shown in Figure 5-4.

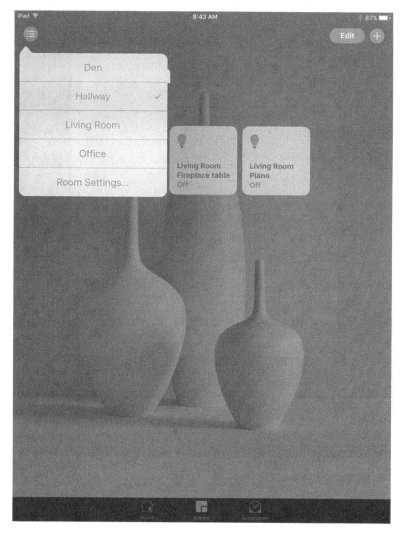

Figure 5-4. Show the list of rooms

To add or remove accessories for a room, tap the room name, and you'll move to that room.

If you want to edit a room's settings, tap Room Settings. You'll see the list of Rooms in a different format as shown in Figure 5-5.

Figure 5-5. Choose a room to edit

Tap the disclosure triangle at the right of the room you want to edit. (Remember, you're editing the room's description: to edit the accessories in a room, just select the room from the list in the top left.) You'll see the view shown in Figure 5-6. Here's where you can rename the room, choose the wallpaper (or take a photo of the actual room to use as a background), or even remove the room from HomeKit.

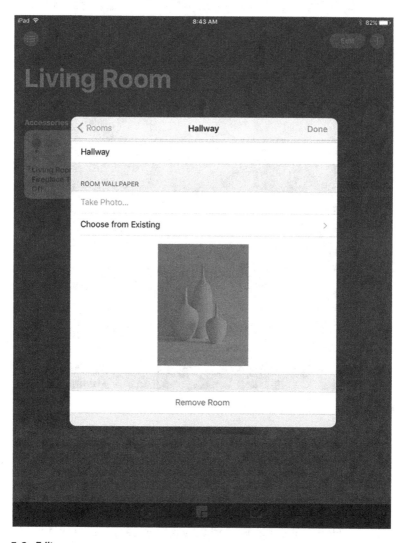

Figure 5-6. Edit a room

To edit an accessory in a room (you'll see how to add an accessory shortly), press and hold the accessory. (If you just tap it, you'll turn the accessory on or off.) Figure 5-7 shows the Details view.

Figure 5-7. Edit accessories in a room

The Details view for an accessory depends on the accessory: HomeKit displays whatever the accessory provides. (Supporting these accessories in code is the topic of the next two chapters.)

To edit the details of an accessory, tap Details in the lower right of the view shown in Figure 5-7 to open the details shown in Figure 5-8. These are mostly the HomeKit settings, and they're basically the same for all accessories. Here is where you can move an accessory from one room to another (just tap Location to get a list to choose from). You can also choose to show this accessory in Favorites on the home screen.

The Status button will let you choose whether this accessory will be shown in the overview items.

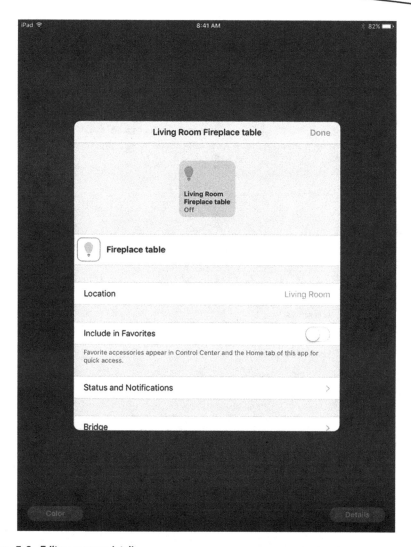

Figure 5-8. Edit accessory details

If you have added a hub such as the Hue bridge, here is where you can configure it as you can see in Figure 5-9.

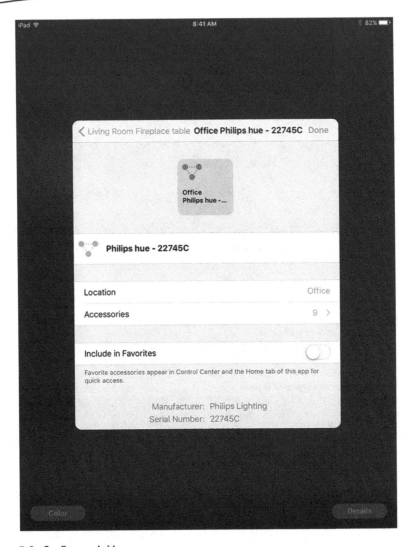

Figure 5-9. Configure a bridge

Merely connecting the bridge according to the manufacturer's instructions may be sufficient at this point. If the hub accessories don't show up, here is where you start to troubleshoot. You may need to compare HomeKit documentation with documentation from the hub manufacturer. Online help on web sites and Twitter can be very helpful. Just be calm and remember that many people by now have managed the connection between the hub and HomeKit.

Using Automation

The Automation tab in the bottom toolbar is the heart of HomeKit's power. It lets you manage *automations*—sequences of commands that can affect one or more accessories (e.g., the accessories in a room). Begin by tapping the Automation tab as shown in Figure 5-10.

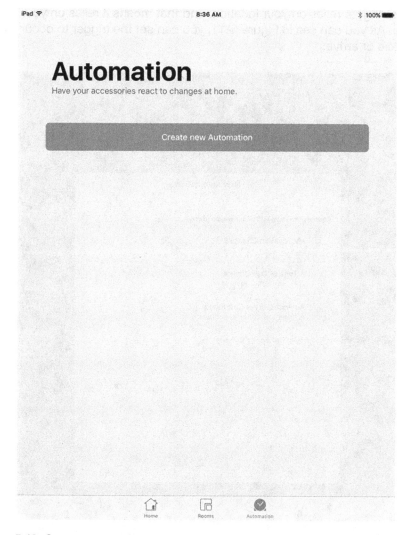

Figure 5-10. Create an automation

Automations come in three varieties as you'll see on the next screen (shown in Figure 5-11). Although they appear different, they really are the same: it's only the triggering event that differs. (That event is called a *trigger* for that reason.)

Automating Location Changes

The first trigger relies on your location, and that means it relies on your iPhone. As you can see in Figure 5-11, you can set the trigger to occur when you leave or arrive.

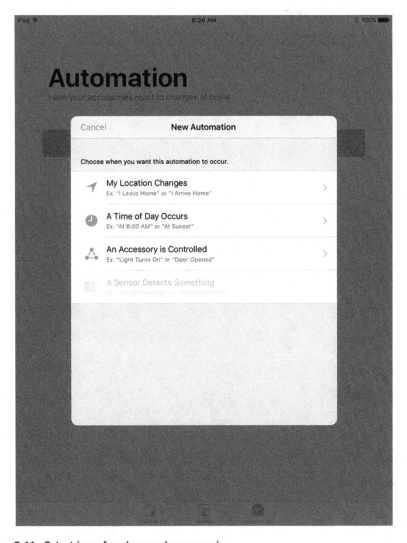

Figure 5-11. Set a trigger for when you leave or arrive

Although the example on the screen shows home, in fact, you can set the automation to any address that you have in Contacts. When you tap Next at the top right, you'll see a list of your contact addresses as shown in Figure 5-12. Just tap the one you want to use.

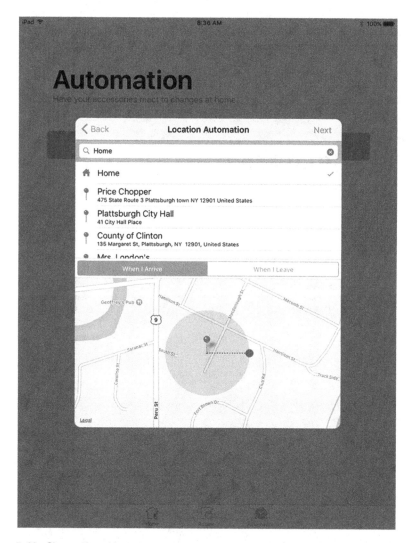

Figure 5-12. Choose the address to use

Automating Time of Day

You can also set an automation to run at a certain time of day (or several days). If you choose that option, you'll be able to add the details as shown in Figure 5-13. Sunrise and sunset are managed for you automatically by Siri and HomeKit, and you can set the time. Most people use automations on a repeat basis, so you can choose the time (or sunrise/sunset) and tap the day(s) on which you want the automation to run. Every Day in the bottom left will do just that.

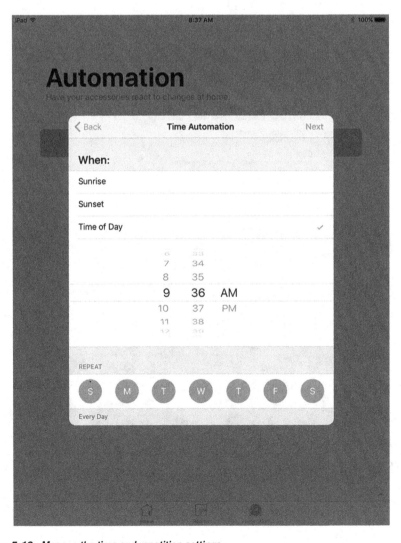

Figure 5-13. Manage the time and repetition settings

Note that this type of automation is designed to repeat. You can use it on a one-time basis, but there is no way to specify a particular date. By default, it will run at the chosen time on the next day you have selected.

Letting Accessories Control Automations

Perhaps the most interesting type of automation is one that is triggered by another accessory. You control this by selecting the accessory in the room that you're interested in as shown in Figure 5-14. (Tap the circle in the top right of an accessory to choose it.)

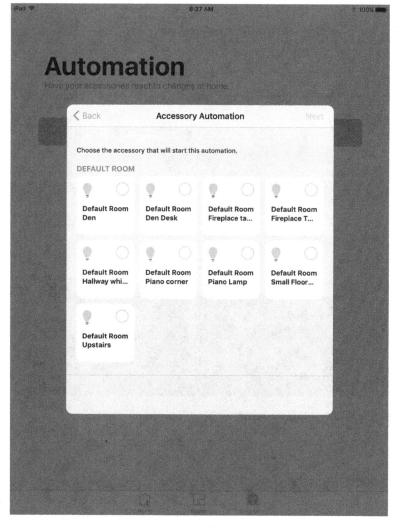

Figure 5-14. Let an accessory trigger an automation

Once you've selected the triggering accessory, set the action it performs that will trigger the automation as you can see in Figure 5-15. (The actions you can choose from differ for each type of accessory.)

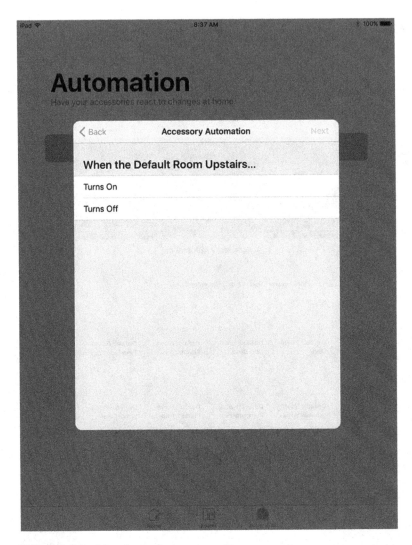

Figure 5-15. Select the triggering action

You have the accessory and the action that you want to trigger your automation. On the next screen select the accessory (or accessories with multiple choices) you want to respond to that trigger as shown in Figure 5-16. (Scenes are described later on, but they basically work the same way as accessories in this context.)

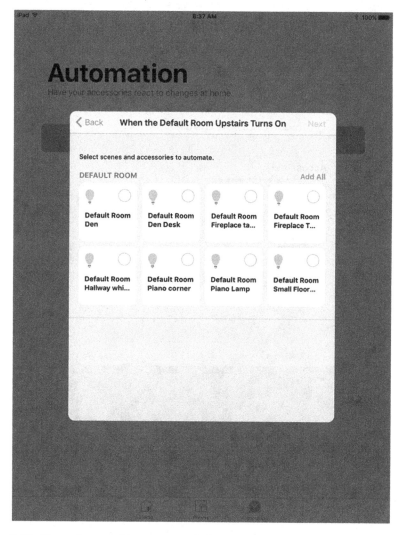

Figure 5-16. Choose the scene(s) or accessory(ies) to automate

The last step is to provide the details of what this automation should do with what accessory(ies) on the next screen, shown in Figure 5-17.

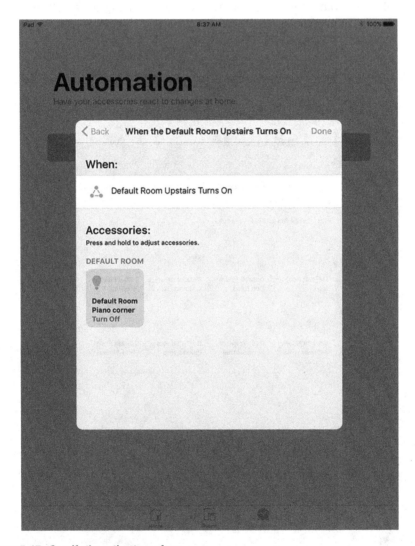

Figure 5-17. Specify the action to perform

Bringing It Together

You've now seen the HomeKit setup process described in terms of how you set it up. If it seems complicated, consider looking at it in reverse, and you'll see how the pieces fit together. Once it is set up, here's what will happen:

1. **Perform** an automation action: turn lights on/off, open a garage door, adjust a thermostat, etc.

2. **When** something happens:

   a. **A time of day**

   b. **Another HomeKit accessory does something**

   c. **You arrive at or leave from a place.**

   The various steps you've gone through in this chapter simply set that up. Along the way, you do have to do some setup actions, but in most cases, you'll reuse them many times. Following are the main setup actions you need to perform:

   - For location-based triggers, make sure the address is in your Contacts. If not, add it.

   - Keep your iPhone with you to let location-based triggers work.

   - Identify each accessory you want to reference either as a trigger or to perform an action.

       - To identify accessories, define them in HomeKit

       - To organize accessories, place them in rooms.

       - To organize accessories regardless of room, mark them as favorites so they appear in the Home tab at the left of the bottom toolbar.

   - Make certain that your hub (Apple TV or iPad) is powered on and linked to WiFi and the Internet and that it's set not to sleep. A surge suppressor is a good idea, but they should recover from momentary power outages.

Exploring the HomeKit World as a Developer, Designer, or Device Manufacturer

So far in this book, you've looked at HomeKit from the outside, observing the things you see and control with HomeKit. Now it's time to look at HomeKit from the inside out by starting with the code. The code is what interacts with the home itself and its components, including third-party devices. Everything talks to code, and in many ways, the code itself if the best description of the HomeKit components. This chapter gives you an overview of the HomeKit framework with its objects and functionality.

HomeKit is a modern framework from Apple, and it's based on Swift. If you're a long-time Swift developer (that means you've used it for two or three years!) you'll be right at home. If you're new to Swift, explore the free Swift iBook that you can download from https://itunes.apple.com/us/book/swift-programming-language/id881256329?mt=11#.

This chapter explores the basics you'll need to use HomeKit. It's designed as a reference so consider reading the first section and then coming back to the other sections as necessary. Once you have the overview of HomeKit, it's a lot easier to learn the details while you're actually trying to do something.

© Jesse Feiler 2016
J. Feiler, *Learn Apple HomeKit on iOS*, DOI 10.1007/978-1-4842-1527-2_6

No matter what part of the HomeKit world you're exploring, the code is the heart of it all. The third-party opportunities for HomeKit are just being explored now. Home is the iOS app that is built into the iOS 10 distribution. More complex and customized versions of that app can easily be imagined. For device manufacturers, there are obvious opportunities in building devices and configuration details that are very specific to the device and its application. Integration of HomeKit technology with other technologies, devices, and construction projects is still a wide-open field.

Before you can explore these and other opportunities, here's the code side of HomeKit that you'll be working with.

HomeKit Overview

If you're experienced with object-oriented programming, this section may bring you sufficiently up to speed to use Swift with HomeKit. It's far from a complete tutorial on either one (developer.apple.com is the source for all definitive documentation), but it can get you going. This section gives you the key features you need to know that are different from what you may already know about object-oriented programming in other languages.

Swift's Object-Oriented Features for HomeKit

Like most object-oriented frameworks in any language, HomeKit consists primarily of *objects* and *functions*. To hone in on the technology a little bit, objects are the runtime instantiations of *classes*. In other words, HomeKit consists of classes that are created at runtime as objects.

Functions are declared either within a class or independently. (In very strict object-oriented coding, free-standing functions are frowned upon, but you can create them.)

A function that is declared within a class is often referred to as a *method*.

There are historical reasons for this terminology, but don't worry about it.

HomeKit classes often represent physical objects (homes, rooms, accessories); they also can represent activities or processes. This is the same as it is in many object-oriented systems, but HomeKit is a bit more focused on physical objects than many other systems. It shouldn't matter to you too much.

Protocols and Delegates: Architecture

One of the things that distinguishes Swift from many other object-oriented programming languages is its use of *protocols* and *delegates*. As in all object-oriented programming languages, a class can be descended from another. The descendent class inherits the functionality and variables of the ancestor (or superclass). This can be overridden in the subclass as needed.

One of the major challenges in object-oriented programming has been the issue of *multiple inheritance*—how do you handle the situation where you want a bit of this class as a superclass and a bit of that class as a superclass —both for the same subclass. Swift manages this with *protocols*. When you declare a class, you specify a class from which it inherits if one exists. There is a common base class for most objects in the Cocoa frameworks (Cocoa Touch and Cocoa), and that base class is NSObject. You can explore NSObject to see its structure and components in the Xcode documentation, but for your purposes now you need merely know that it's the common base class for many of the Cocoa classes.

If you want to mix and match parts of several classes to create a form of multiple inheritance, you can use *protocols*. A protocol has some resemblance to classes in that its definition can contain methods, but a protocol is not directly instantiated as a class is. Instead, a class can declare that it *conforms* to a protocol. That means that the class itself implements the protocol (strictly speaking, the required methods of a protocol because some methods can be marked as optional). If a class conforms to a protocol, its subclasses conform to that protocol as well. The class or its subclasses must implement the methods declared in the protocol. The syntax for declaring classes, superclasses, and protocols makes the commonality clear. For example, following is a declaration of a Swift class:

```
class MyClass {
}
```

Here is the declaration of a class that will be used as a superclass. Note that there's nothing syntactical to indicate that it will be a superclass: that's just for clarity of the code example.

```
class MySuperClass {
}
```

Following is a declaration of a Swift class with a superclass:

```
class MyClass2: MySuperClass {
}
```

Here is a declaration of a protocol.

```
protocol MyProtocol {
   var protocolVar: String {get}
}
```

The protocol is never going to be implemented on its own as a class could be. Thus, when declaring a property protocolVar that is a string, the protocol will rely on a class that actually adopts the protocol to implement protocolVar.

Following is a declaration of a Swift class which adopts a protocol:

```
class MyClass3: MyProtocol {
}
```

Here is a declaration of a Swift class with a superclass where the Swift class adopts a protocol.

```
class MyClass4: MySuperClass, MyProtocol {
  internal var protocolVar: String = "Test"
}
```

It is the class that adopts the protocol that implements it, so after the previous code snippets, you can now write the following:

```
let x = MyClass4 ()
print (x.protocolVar)
```

Figure 6-1 shows this code all put together.

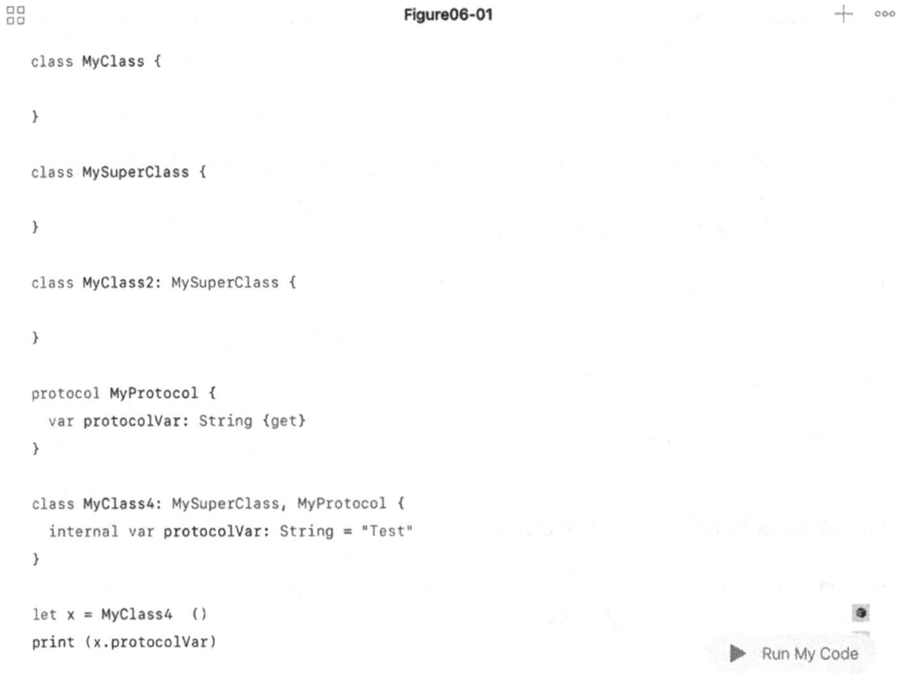

```
                                        Figure06-01                              +  ooo

  class MyClass {

  }

  class MySuperClass {

  }

  class MyClass2: MySuperClass {

  }

  protocol MyProtocol {
    var protocolVar: String {get}
  }

  class MyClass4: MySuperClass, MyProtocol {
    internal var protocolVar: String = "Test"
  }

  let x = MyClass4  ()
  print (x.protocolVar)                                          ▶ Run My Code
```

Figure 6-1. Classes, superclasses, and protocols example

In case you're wondering how the compiler can correctly interpret a line of code such as the following, where `MySomething` could be either a protocol or a superclass, the answer is that the compiler requires that `MySomething` be declared before use, and it can figure out which it is.

```
class MyClass: MySomething {
}
```

It is a commonly used convention (or design pattern if you prefer that terminology) that when a class adopts a protocol, the protocol functionality may in fact be implemented by another object at runtime. This object is the *delegate*. This structure keeps the functionality well-organized and makes development and maintenance of code easier.

By using protocols, the multiple inheritance issue is pretty much solved. In addition, by being able to add protocols to implement rather limited functionalities, the inheritance tree in Swift is often much flatter than in other languages. In fact, many protocols in Swift are particularly lightweight and are added to a number of classes as needed. The next section examines three protocols that appear over and over in HomeKit classes.

Protocols and Delegates: Key Players

As noted previously, Swift class hierarchies that use protocols tend to be much flatter than class hierarchies in other languages. The common base object for Cocoa and Cocoa Touch (`NSObject`) which itself conforms to `NSObjectProtocol` does a lot of the heavy lifting for many objects in the frameworks. Most of the HomeKit classes are subclasses of `NSObject` (and therefore conform to `NSObjectProtocol`).

In addition, many of the HomeKit classes also adopt three very common protocols: `CVarArg`, `Equatable`, and `Hashable`. You don't really need to worry about them, but if you're looking things up in the documentation and keep running across them, here's what they are and what they do.

`CVarArg`

This protocol allows you to use a variadic list of variables (a C va_list).

`Equatable`

This protocolSwift's Object-Oriented featuresprotocols and delegateskey players means that types can be compared with == or !=.

`Hashable`

As its name suggests, this protocol means that objects conforming to it can be hashed so that you an easily locate them in a dictionary or a set.

Creating New Instances

You'll find that many of the HomeKit classes do not allow you to simply create new instances of themselves. You must use a method that returns a new instance in some context. These are often referred to as "factory methods."

For example, if you want to create a new room, you use addRoom (withName: completionHandler:) on an HMHome instance. This means that the room you add is added to the rooms array in the HMHome instance.

This design pattern is repeated in many places (e.g., HMZone instances). This may minimize the issue of "orphan" objects.

Basic HomeKit Objects

The basic objects in a home are

- Rooms

- Accessories

- Scenes

- Actions (these are organized into action sets which will be described later in this section)

They are the main objects you'll be working with (in addition to the home itself, of course). Within an HMHome instance, you can find them in arrays.

The balance of this chapter explores those objects. You'll see the interface as well as the code that can be used to implement it. (Note that the actual implementation within the Home app may use other code, but it will functionally be the same as the code you see here.)

Almost every object in HomeKit has a unique identifier:

```
var uniqueIdentifier: UUID
```

A unique identifier is a string that is generated in such a way as to be unique. (The example shown in Apple documentation is

```
E621E1F8-C36C-495A-93FC-0C247A3E6E5F)
```

Swift UUID (universally unique identifier) is bridged to NSUUID so the two can be used interchangeably. It is based on RFC 4122 version 4 random bytes.

Working with Rooms

Rooms are what you work with when you set up HomeKit as a user, but here is the back-end view.

Managing Rooms

Add a room by tapping the list icon at the top left of any room in the Home app as you see in Figure 6-2.

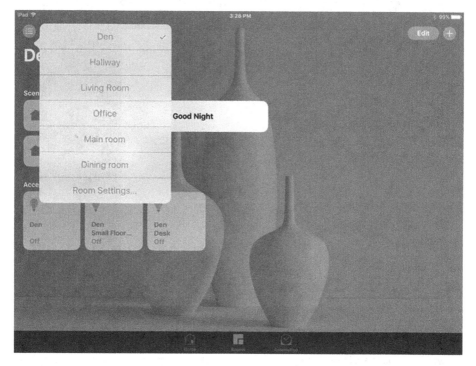

Figure 6-2. Listing and adding rooms

As you see in the background of Figure 6-2, this list of rooms is available from any room.

The list of rooms is an array of the rooms in an HMHome, so that must be in the view you see in Figure 6-2. The list is found using the HMHome array: HMRoom array

```
var rooms: [HMRoom]
```

Thus, in order to add a room, you can tell from the interface that you know the HMHome object (because that's where the list of rooms is). The HMHome class manages adding and removing rooms from the home using the following:

```
func addRoom(withName: String, completionHandler: (HMRoom?, Error?) -> Void)
func removeRoom(HMRoom, completionHandler: (Error?) -> Void)
```

Figure 6-3 shows how you add a room.

Figure 6-3. Room settings

There's another interesting aspect of the HMHome API (application program interface) that relates to rooms, and that's a method that returns all parts of the home that aren't in any other room.

```
func roomForEntireHome()
```

So you can be confident in proceeding under the assumption that objects such as accessories will be in a room even if it's only the entire home room.

Editing a Room

Once you have added or located a room, you can edit it. Figure 6-4 shows the interface (you get here as a user from Add Room at the bottom of Figure 6-3).

The name of a room is set when you first create it using `HMHome`
`addRoom(withName: String, completionHandler: (HMRoom?, Error?) -> Void)`

Updating the name after you have created the room is done with HMRoom

```
func updateName(String, completionHandler: (Error?) -> Void)
```

Figure 6-4 shows the user interface.

The same design pattern that has an array of rooms within a home occurs with accessories in a room: they are stored in an array in HMRoom.

```
var accessories: [HMAccessory]
```

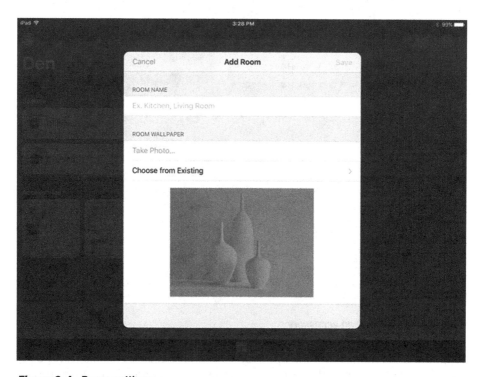

Figure 6-4. Room settings

Working with Accessories

Rooms within a home are a fairly simple case if only because both the home and the room are physical objects, and in practice rooms are fairly static. When you think about it, changes to rooms within a home are frequently changes in name (e.g., the nursery becomes the study). It's true that accessories are a different matter if only because they tend to move around. (The lamp that used to be in the living room may be moved to a bedroom.)

Finding Accessories

The HMAccessoryBrowser class is used to find accessories. If you've set up a HomeKit home, you've been through the process. You start by adding an accessory, as you can see in Figure 6-5.

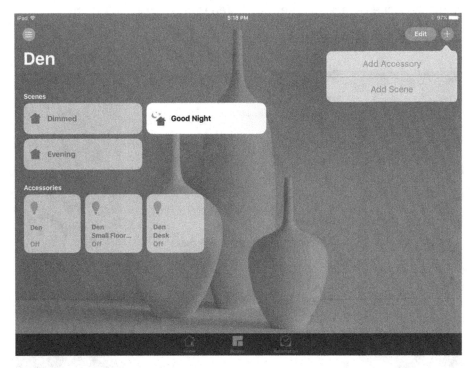

Figure 6-5. Selecting an accessory

What happens next is that the app launches an HMAccessoryBrowser. It goes around and attempts to discover accessories as you can see in Figure 6-6.

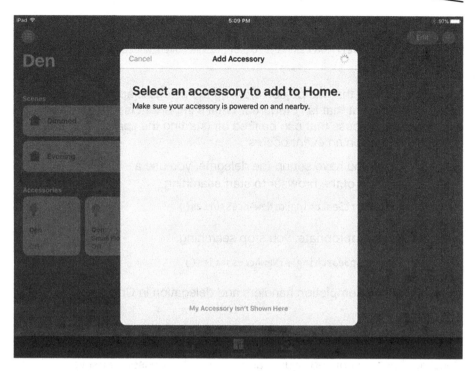

Figure 6-6. Browsing for accessories

The process that goes on is a typical Cocoa design pattern involving a delegate. There are three steps.

1. First, you start searching for accessories that are not yet associated with a home. (If accessories are associated with a home, the user will need to remove them.) To carry out the search, you create an HMAccessory Browser.

2. When an accessory is found, you need to be notified. In some cases, a completion routine is used for this call-back processing. However, in other cases (such as this), a *delegate* is used. The delegate implements a protocol—in this case, it's the HMAccessoryBrowserDelegateProtocol. The protocol consists of two methods:

```
func accessoryBrowser(HMAccessoryBrowser, didFindNewAccessory: HMAccessory)
```

```
func accessoryBrowser(HMAccessoryBrowser, didRemoveNewAccessory:
HMAccessory)
```

It is fairly common that the object creating the delegate appoints itself as the delegate, but that isn't requred. What's important is that this is an asynchronous process that can be fired off (starting the search) and then handled if and when an event occurs.

1. Once you have set up the delegate, you use a method of the browser to start searching.

   ```
   func startSearchingForNewAccessories()
   ```

2. When appropriate, you stop searching.

   ```
   func stopSearchingForNewAccessories()
   ```

There is more on completion handlers and delegation in Chapter 7.

Managing Accessories

Once you have completed your search, you add accessories using HMHome.

```
func addAccessory(_ accessory: HMAccessory,
  completionHandler completion: (Error?) -> Void)
```

Not surprisingly, you remove them also using HMHome.

```
func removeAccessory(_ accessory: HMAccessory,
  completionHandler completion: (Error?) -> Void)
```

You can get a list of accessories from a room using the HMRoom method that returns the array of that room's accessories.

```
var accessories: [HMAccessory]
```

Because accessories are added and removed by HMHome, you can move them around using HMHome:

```
func assignAccessory(_ accessory: HMAccessory,
  to room: HMRoom,
  completionHandler completion: (Error?) -> Void)
```

Editing Accessories

You see the accessory information in a view that varies depending on the type of accessory. For example, if you tap and hold an accessory in Figure 6-5, you may see the view shown in Figure 6-7 which represents a light bulb.

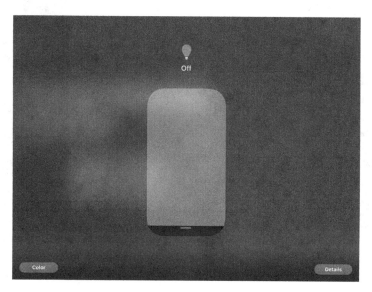

Figure 6-7. Editing an accessory's details

As far as the interface of the Home app is concerned, you can edit an accessory's general information that is visible to the room itself by a long press on it in the user interface. Figures 6-8 and 6-9 show you the user interface. It is the same for all types of accessories.

Figure 6-8. Setting the values (top)

Figure 6-9. Setting the values (bottom)

Note   Chapter 7 provides much more on accessories.

Dive into Accessories

When it comes to home automation, the basics are homes, rooms, and devices. This applies to any home automation environment. Generally, you can adjust the settings on the devices (most often bulbs for many people), and you can combine devices with their settings into scenes. A timing mechanism lets you turn scenes on and off.

HomeKit goes beyond the basics in two important ways.

■ HomeKit is built as a home for third-party devices and apps. Apple is starting with the framework and the database and building it out for others to flesh out. At this point (and, rumor has it, for the future), Apple is not developing HomeKit devices. For those of us who are into software design, starting from the logic first is a great way to work (it's what we do every day). Apple's involvement with the hardware for home automation consists of its certification program for devices that work with HomeKit.

■ HomeKit is positioned as a component of the Apple devices on which it is pre-installed. The Home app is part of iOS 10, so it's ready for anyone who wants to connect devices to it.

Chapter 6 describes the devices for home automation fairly generically. You've seen the code to add accessories to rooms and how to add rooms to homes, but the basic code there doesn't require too much exploration inside the HomeKit classes that support accessories.

This chapter goes inside accessories. They are the features of HomeKit that actually provide the user benefits, and they are implemented in simple, elegant, and powerful classes.

© Jesse Feiler 2016
J. Feiler, *Learn Apple HomeKit on iOS*, DOI 10.1007/978-1-4842-1527-2_7

Rooms within a home are a fairly simple case if only because both the home and the room are physical objects, and in practice rooms are fairly static. When you think about it, changes to rooms within a home are frequently changes in name (e.g., the nursery becomes the study). It's true that accessories are a different matter if only because they tend to move around. (That lamp that used to be in the living room may be moved to a bedroom.)

Building Accessories

In order to build actual accessories (rather than buying pre-built accessories online or in a store), you need to join the MFi program. Once you are licensed, you will have access to HomeKit technical specifications (i.e., physical specifications as opposed to the API specifications that you get as a registered developer). You also have access to hardware technical support and marketing materials (e.g., the MFi logo). Find out more at the MFi FAQ page: `https://mfi.apple.com/MFiWeb/getFAQ.action`.

Working with Accessories

You have seen the basics of what an accessory is in this book so far. In Chapter 6, you've also seen the basics of the API (application program interface) to set up an accessory. Beyond that, the best way to learn what an accessory is to create one using the HomeKit Accessory Simulator. (Remember that the accessory itself may not yet exist if you're working on a development project that combines new accessories with a new HomeKit app.)

There are two key questions you have to answer about your accessories.

- What is the accessory—its name and some descriptive information about it?

- What does the accessory do? Obviously, this is related to what it is, but it is not always clear just from the description of the accessory. In HomeKit terms, what *service* does the accessory provide?

If you are going to be developing an app for HomeKit (perhaps a version of the Home app that is focused on your particular functionality and issues as you'll see in Chapter 8), you can simulate accessories without buying them (or even before they have been fully developed). Get started by following the instructions on the Developer Site to download the HomeKit Accessory Simulator from `https://developer.apple.com/library/prerelease/content/documentation/NetworkingInternet/Conceptual/HomeKitDeveloperGuide/TestingYourHomeKitApp/TestingYourHomeKitApp.html`.

When you create a new accessory in the HomeKit Accessory Simulator, you see the view shown in Figure 7-1.

What Is an Accessory?

Create a new accessory by launching the HomeKit Accessory Simulator and choosing File ➤ New ➤ Accessory to open the modal view shown in Figure 7-1.You can also create a new bridge, but the accessory choice is the most common one.

Figure 7-1. Create a new accessory with HomeKit Accessory Simulator

You can read this section as a how-to of how to build an accessory in the simulator, but you can also read it as the ultimate definition of what an accessory is. In that view, remember that the accessory also has the following properties:

```
var uniqueIdentifier: UUID
var uniqueIdentifiersForBridgedAccessories: [UUID]?
```

As you do in other cases, you assign a delegate to an accessory (it is optional so not every accessory has a delegate). You might have a delegate for each accessory or one for all of them. Whatever the delegate is, it implements these methods. As you can see, the accessory's delegate finds out when there are changes so whatever is needed to be done can be done. The delegate implements the HMAccessoryDelegate protocol,

```
func accessoryDidUpdateName(HMAccessory)
func accessoryDidUpdateReachability(HMAccessory)
func accessoryDidUpdateServices(HMAccessory)
func accessory(HMAccessory, didUpdateNameFor: HMService)
func accessory(HMAccessory, service: HMService, didUpdateValueFor:
HMCharacteristic)
func accessory(HMAccessory, didUpdateAssociatedServiceTypeFor: HMService),
```

Basic Accessory Data

You fill in the basic accessory information at the top section of the accessory view shown in Figure 7-1. What it does will be described as the services that you can add with the button at the bottom of Figure 7-1. This section focuses on the description—the Accessory information shown in Figure 7-1.

You start with the setup code that is created for you by the simulator, but as your testing continues, you can modify it. Pairings are used during testing as well. The basic information shown here is up to you.

Categories

Choose a category for the accessory. The interface provides you with the list shown in Figure 7-2.

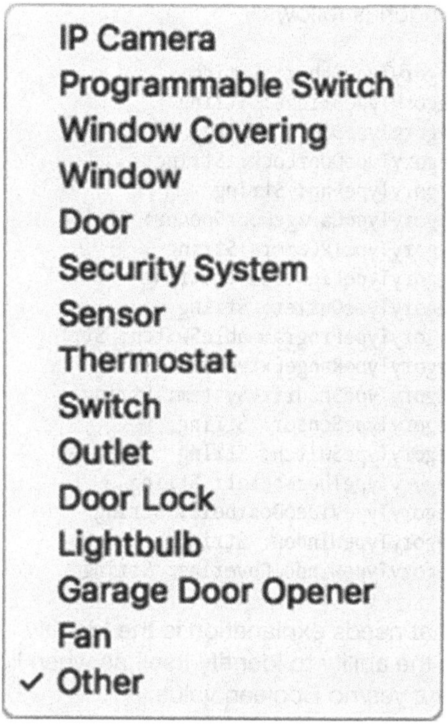

IP Camera
Programmable Switch
Window Covering
Window
Door
Security System
Sensor
Thermostat
Switch
Outlet
Door Lock
Lightbulb
Garage Door Opener
Fan
✓ Other

Figure 7-2. *Choose a category*

The code for the categories follows:

```
let HMAccessoryCategoryTypeOther: String
let HMAccessoryCategoryTypeBridge: String
let HMAccessoryCategoryTypeDoor: String
let HMAccessoryCategoryTypeDoorLock: String
let HMAccessoryCategoryTypeFan: String
let HMAccessoryCategoryTypeGarageDoorOpener: String
let HMAccessoryCategoryTypeIPCamera:String
let HMAccessoryCategoryTypeLightbulb: String
let HMAccessoryCategoryTypeOutlet: String
let HMAccessoryCategoryTypeProgrammableSwitch: String
let HMAccessoryCategoryTypeRangeExtender: String
let HMAccessoryCategoryTypeSecuritySystem: String
let HMAccessoryCategoryTypeSensor: String
let HMAccessoryCategoryTypeSwitch: String
let HMAccessoryCategoryTypeThermostat: String
let HMAccessoryCategoryTypeVideoDoorbell: String
let HMAccessoryCategoryTypeWindow: String
let HMAccessoryCategoryTypeWindowCovering: String
```

The only category that needs explanation is the Identify information: does this accessory have the ability to identify itself as when light bulb flickers to identify itself. This is a yes/no Boolean value.

- Name
- Manufacturer
- Model
- Serial Number
- Identify
- Accessory Categories

Characteristics

You add characteristics that apply to this accessory. You can add as many characteristics as you want to an accessory. You use the Add Characteristic button shown in Figure 7-1. It opens the modal view shown in Figure 7-3. The details shown in Figure 7-3 depend on what type of characteristic you select at the top of the view.

Figure 7-3. Choose a characteristic

Type

For the characteristic, choose its type from the pop-up menu at the top of Figure 7-3. Figure 7-4 shows the choices.

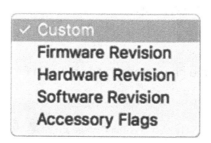

Figure 7-4. Characteristic choices

Format

Choose the format for the characteristic as shown in Figure 7-5.

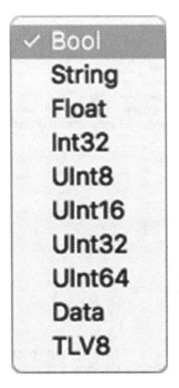

Figure 7-5. *Units for the characteristic*

Units

Choose the units for the characteristic as shown in Figure 7-6.

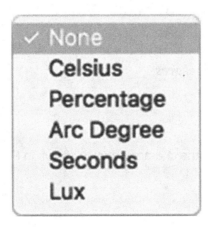

Figure 7-6. *Units for the characteristic*

What Does the Accessory Do? (Services)

Add as many services as you want to your accessory by using the Add Service . . . button at the bottom of Figure 7-1. When you add a service, you need to complete the information shown in Figure 7-7.

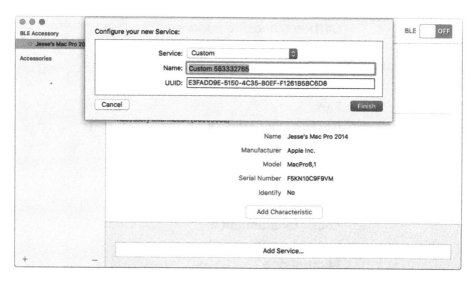

Figure 7-7. Configure a service

Note that you can assign a specific UUID (universally unique identifier) to the service. Figure 7-8 shows the choices for the type of service.

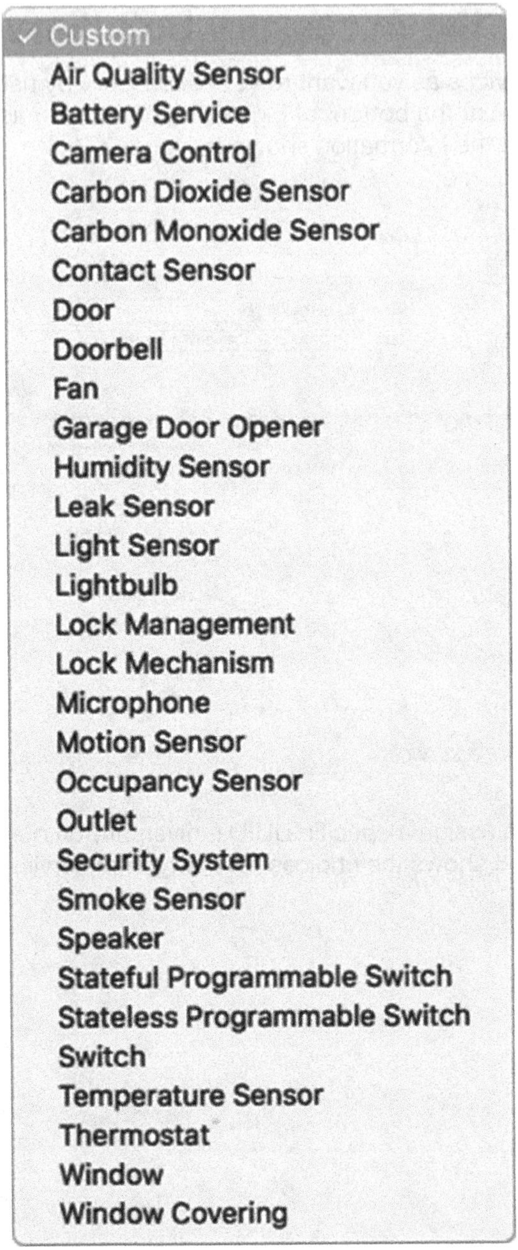

✓ Custom
Air Quality Sensor
Battery Service
Camera Control
Carbon Dioxide Sensor
Carbon Monoxide Sensor
Contact Sensor
Door
Doorbell
Fan
Garage Door Opener
Humidity Sensor
Leak Sensor
Light Sensor
Lightbulb
Lock Management
Lock Mechanism
Microphone
Motion Sensor
Occupancy Sensor
Outlet
Security System
Smoke Sensor
Speaker
Stateful Programmable Switch
Stateless Programmable Switch
Switch
Temperature Sensor
Thermostat
Window
Window Covering

Figure 7-8. Select a service

Finding Accessory State

The following are transient characteristics of accessories that depend on the network and other conditions. You manage them in the API rather than the simulator. The simulator gives you basic data that is then modified, and such modifications are passed on to the accessory's delegate. You need to set that delegate when you create the accessory in your code.

These are the most commonly used functions to query an accessory's state in general. You can query other properties specifically as you need them, but these are the state properties.

```
var isReachable: Bool
var isBlocked: Bool
var isBridged: Bool
```

Setting Preferences for the HomeKit Accessory Simulator

Finally, note that you can set preferences for the simulator to use as shown in Figure 7-9.

Figure 7-9. *Set HomeKit Accessory Simulator Preferences*

Chapter 8

Imaginative Opportunities: Events, Triggers, and Actions

Your homes and rooms with their accessories along with the accessory characteristics and services are a great way of organizing your HomeKit assets, but on their own, they really don't do anything. They just sit there waiting for you to activate them with Siri commands or with . . . something else? (Note that Siri is an interface that can work with your HomeKit assets, but its use is more of a user interface concern than development, so it's not covered in this book.)

What brings your HomeKit assets and resources to life and makes your home "smart" is the trio of *events*, *triggers*, and *actions*. These aren't physical devices: they are concepts or abstractions that represent what you want to *do* with your HomeKit resources as well as *when* you want to do those things. Although those words represent specific aspects of the HomeKit API (specifically HMEvent, HMTrigger, and HMAction) they are used in their everyday meaning. In this book when the API (application program interface) names such as HMEvent are used, they are shown in a distinctive font.

The basic pattern is simple. You define an event (such a specific time of day or arriving at a location), and a trigger watches for that event to occur. When it does occur, the trigger launches an action. This is how "when I get home, turn hallway scene on" happens.

WHERE ARE SCENES?

A scene is something a user sets up that combines accessories and settings. Thus, "hallway scene" might consist of hallway ceiling light being turned on to a specific color and brightness as well as opening the hallway window blinds. It is the user who creates the scenes: They are based on the API that is discussed in Chapters 6 and 7. From the developer's point of view, a scene is a collection of actions: an *action set*.

Events, actions, and triggers work together. You may want to scan this chapter quickly to get the big picture and then come back to focus on specifics. This is a case where a test installation of perhaps a single lamp can be very helpful in getting a feel for HomeKit. As you experiment, remember that triggers are not instantaneous when you set them. You can get an instantaneous response when you turn a scene on or off, but when you connect scenes to events and triggers, there can be a time lag as HomeKit establishes the settings and then implements them. Users sometimes wait for a while (often a day) to check that their events and triggers are set properly as time goes along and daily events occur.

Working with Events

Events are often things that happen outside the world of HomeKit (often, but not always). They fall into two groups which are subclasses of HMEvent. The subclasses are HMLocationEvent and HMCharacteristicEvent. HMEvent itself contains a universally unique identifier (UUID) called uniqueIdentifier. Any other properties are properties of subclasses. As you'll see when you start to use events in triggers, this abstract superclass is a key component of triggers because although geofencing is very different from the state of an accessory's data, both geofencing and characteristics are the same when they become part of triggers.

> **Tip**   You may want to think of an event as a *noun*—that is, a *thing*.

Geofencing with Location Events

A location event is a geofence event. Its basic property is a CLRegion (i.e., a region as defined in CLLocationManager in the Core Location framework).

The heart of an HMLocationEvent is its region which is represented by its sole property.

```
var region: CLRegion?
```

You create an HMLocation event with a region, and you can update that region as necessary.

```
init(region: CLRegion)
func updateRegion(_ region: CLRegion, completionHandler completion: (Error?)
-> Void)
```

Monitoring Characteristic Events

A characteristic event is an event that represents a certain value of an accessory characteristic. For example, a characteristic event for a door lock could be that it is locked or unlocked. A characteristic event for a smoke detector could be that it senses smoke. And, very simply, a characteristic event for a light bulb could be that it is on or off.

> **Tip**   You may want to think of a characteristic as an adjective—that is, a
> *modifier* or *description* of an object.

Thus for an HMCharacteristicEvent, two properties are involved: the characteristic (lock) and the value that you care about (secured/unsecured).

The two properties of HMCharacteristicEvent are

```
var characteristic: HMCharacteristic
var triggerValue: TriggerValueType?
```

You can initialize an HMCharacteristicEvent with a characteristic and an optional value. Because triggerValue can be null, you can come back later on (or the user can come back) to specify a value (that is what "optional" means in Swift — it can have no value). A binary condition such as secured/unsecured doesn't lend itself to this, but a temperature sensor certainly does.

```
init(characteristic: HMCharacteristic, triggerValue: TriggerValueType?)
func updateTriggerValue(_ triggerValue: TriggerValueType?, completionHandler
completion: (Error?) -> Void)
```

Working with Triggers

Triggers execute action sets (HMActionSet) which themselves consist of actions (they're described in the following section). HMTrigger is an abstract class: You typically implement (or subclass) one of the primary HMTrigger subclasses—HMTimerTrigger or HMEventTrigger. Triggers are said to *fire* when a certain event occurs (i.e., when you enter or leave the region of an HMLocationEvent or when a characteristic of an accessory in an HMCharacteristicEvent takes on the trigger value you're waiting for.)

Triggers are identified by names and UUIDs. Both are created when a trigger is created. Names can be updated as needed (the update function allows a delegate to notice that the name has been changed).

```
var name: String
func updateName(_ name: String, completionHandler completion: (Error?) ->
Void)
var uniqueIdentifier: UUID
```

In addition to the static name and UUID, it's important to control whether or not a trigger is enabled and the last time it fired:

```
var isEnabled: Bool
func enable(_ enable: Bool, completionHandler completion: (Error?) -> Void)
var lastFireDate: Date?
```

> **Note** lastFireDate is an optional because the trigger may never have been fired. Also, remember that the Date type is actually a bridge to NSDate in the Foundation framework. NSDate is a single point in time and is not specific to a calendar, time zone, or location.

Using a Basic Trigger

The action sets for a trigger are managed by the following methods:

```
var actionSets: [HMActionSet]
func addActionSet(_ actionSet: HMActionSet, completionHandler completion:
(Error?) -> Void)
func removeActionSet(_ actionSet: HMActionSet, completionHandler completion:
(Error?) -> Void)
```

Adding Conditions to Triggers with Predicates

Event triggers can use *predicates* to add conditions that must be true for the event trigger to fire.

Predicates are a basic part of the Cocoa and Cocoa Touch foundation framework. They are a way of describing a Boolean condition to use in retrieving data from a data store or for any other case in which you need a Boolean such as defining a condition for an event trigger.

Working with Actions

As a developer or designer, you generally deal with actions in order to set up the user interface that allows users to put them together so that they can be triggered by events. The actual running of an action or action set happens when the trigger fires. An action can be used to turn an accessory on or off or to adjust its characteristics (such as brightness or color).

> **Tip**   You may want to think of an action as a *verb*—that is, an action in the common everyday use of the word.

Most of the time, you work with *action sets* (HMActionSet) which themselves consist of sets of actions (HMAction).

> **Note**   *Set* is used in its technical sense of an unordered collection of items. This means that the actions within an action set will execute in an unspecified order. It is sometimes the case that those actions will execute in the order in which they have been specified, but that is happenstance. This can be important in tracking down apparent bugs.)

Action sets have names and UUIDs. Siri recognizes the names of action sets. Your code makes it possible for users to build on it in creating their own HomeKit environments.

Action sets consist of actions, but actions are specific subclasses of HMAction. HMAction is an abstract class which means that you don't directly create instances of it. You create specific instances of classes such as HMCharacteristicWriteAction which itself writes a specific value to a characteristic of an accessory. Following is the declaration of the method you'll use:

```
init(characteristic: HMCharacteristic, targetValue: TargetValueType)
```

As you saw in Chapter 7, accessories can have characteristics and services. To find a specific service to use in allowing users to set up an action set, you can use a function such as this one to find the services for a given accessory you can use this variable of HMAccessory on the specific accessory the user wants to work with:

```
var services: [HMService] { get }
```

If you don't happen to have the specific accessory when you are writing the characteristic, you can find it with the following method of HMHome, which lets you find services by their type in the entire home:

```
func servicesWithTypes(_ serviceTypes: [String]) -> [HMService]?
```

Note that this function returns an optional: there may be no services of a given type and your code must handle this case.

Services and characteristics are linked to one another, so when you have an HMCharacteristic, you usually have a related service. Likewise, when you have an HMService you can find its characteristics.

Following is the property in HMCharacteristic you can use to get its service:

```
var service: HMService?
```

Starting from an HMService object, here's how you find its accessory:

```
var accessory: HMAccessory?
```

Note that working either from an accessory or a characteristic, you can get the other with the very important caveat that both of these properties are optionals so they may not exist. That would particularly be the case as users are setting up their home and have not yet completed the task in many cases. Don't assume that a user setting up a home tidies up all the loose ends.

There are valid reasons why there may be "orphan" scenes as users are experimenting. Also, remember that you are dealing with devices that have their own issues regarding power and other factors. Although the light bulbs that are manufactured today are estimated to have life spans measured in years—many years—they will eventually fail. Wired connections such as to a power supply or wall outlet are subject to the vicissitudes of cable issues ranging from becoming unplugged to being accidentally plugged into an outlet that is controlled by a switch.

This last is a common issue for many people. You often find a wall outlet with two sockets one of which is controlled by a switch. This means that a wall switch can turn on a light connected to the switched outlet while the other one is always on for a device such as an electric clock, humidifier, or something else that should remain on at all times. You may know this and even remember it over the years, but someone who does a big house-cleaning project may unplug both plugs to move the sofa and your HomeKit-controlled lamp winds up in the switched socket.

Chapter 9

Working with iCloud and Users with HomeKit

HomeKit works with the networks it finds. The most basic level of communication is between an accessory and your HomeKit hub which typically is either an Apple TV or an iPad—or both. For short distances (such as within your home, HomeKit uses a WiFi network or Bluetooth Low Energy (Bluetooth LE).

Beyond the home, HomeKit uses an Apple ID over whatever network it can find. With the advent of iOS 10 and the Home app (pre-installed on iPads), HomeKit is more available than ever.

This chapter helps you use some of the networking capabilities of HomeKit.

Warning   Your hub needs to be powered on at all times for your HomeKit actions to work. Remember that when you define an automation that turns a scene on (see Chapter 8), HomeKit uses the triggers to launch scenes. If you power on a device or hub after a trigger should have fired (or actually did fire but the accessory wasn't powered on), nothing happens until the next trigger opportunity arises. If that's a time of day, the next opportunity is the next day.

© Jesse Feiler 2016
J. Feiler, *Learn Apple HomeKit on iOS*, DOI 10.1007/978-1-4842-1527-2_9

Setting Up Hubs

Your hub needs to be powered on all the time and it needs network connections. For most people, this means making certain that the hub itself (Apple TV or iPad) can use Bluetooth and a WiFi network. For remote access, the hub needs to be connected to the Internet (usually this is via the WiFi connection).

Apple TV

For Apple TV, you need to make certain that HomeKit is enabled. For starters, make certain that the Apple TV uses the same Apple ID you use (or will use) for your HomeKit hub. (This is not an issue for the many people who use a single Apple ID.)

On your Apple TV, go to Settings, as shown in Figure 9-1.

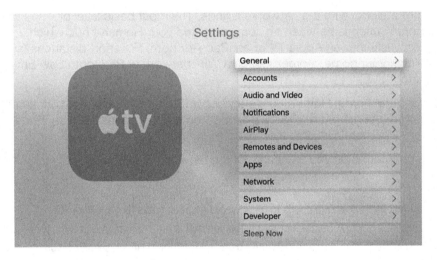

Figure 9-1. Go to Settings on Apple TV

Select Accounts to set up your Apple ID for HomeKit. As you see in Figure 9-2, you need to set an Apple ID for *Home Sharing* (that's the Settings term for HomeKit.)

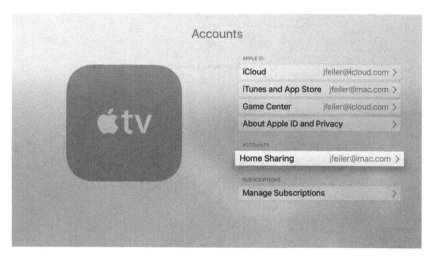

Figure 9-2. Set the Apple ID account

If, at some point in the future, you want to turn off the Apple TV as a hub, turn it off as you see in Figure 9-3 where the Home Sharing account is being turned off.

Figure 9-3. Turn home sharing off

iPad

The process for setting up an iPad as a hub is a little different. Go to Settings on the iPad and then find Home as you see in Figure 9-4. You can have several HomeKit hubs sharing the same Apple ID if you want.

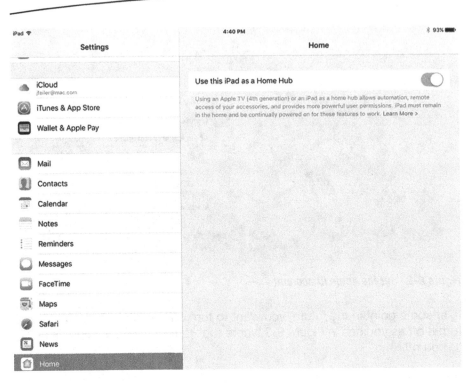

Figure 9-4. Make an iPad a HomeKit hub

Setting Up Users

In addition to your hubs, you can set up users for HomeKit. Everyone who shares the Apple ID you've used to set up HomeKit can log on with his or her own Apple ID, but you can ask other people to join.

Inviting Other Users

From the Home tab in Home on your iPad, tap Edit in the top right and then the disclosure triangle next to the name of the home (it might be "My Home" if you're using the defaults) to open the alert shown in Figure 9-5. Note that you can do this from the same Apple ID as you have used for your Apple TV. Many people rely on Apple TV to do the back-end processing of automations, but they use an iPad to manage things such as adding users. You'll see how to manage what users can do in the section "Setting Permissions for Users."

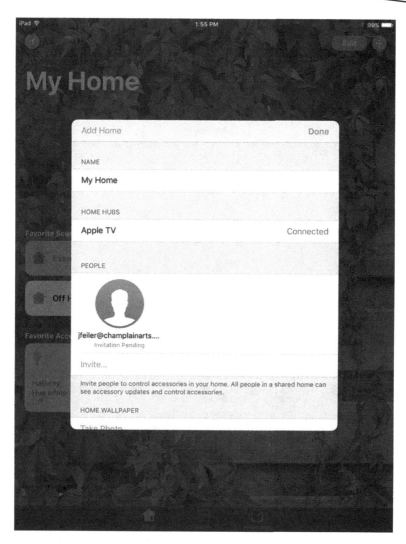

Figure 9-5. *Invite other users*

Click Invite to open the invitation alert shown in Figure 9-6. Type in the e-mail address you want to use for the invitation at the top.

Figure 9-6. *Send the invitation*

Responding to an Invitation

You probably don't know how your invitee will receive the invitation. It can arrive on an iPad or an iPhone, so here are the screens your invitee will see. You'll particularly need this information if you haven't contacted the person before you send the invitation. You might consider contacting the person in advance (after all, it's only polite).

Responding on an iPad

If the invitee receives the invitation, it may appear on the lock screen of the iPad as you see in Figure 9-7. (Notice that it comes as a notification from Home rather than a message or an e-mail. You can tell this from the icon on the notification.)

Figure 9-7. The user receives the invitation

If the user receives the invitation on an iPad, here's what it looks like once the notification of the invitation is unlocked. In the invitee's Settings, the invitation is shown in the Follow Ups section (you may never have seen that before because these invitations havent been used much until now). The invitee can choose to view the invitation (or not) as you see in Figure 9-8.

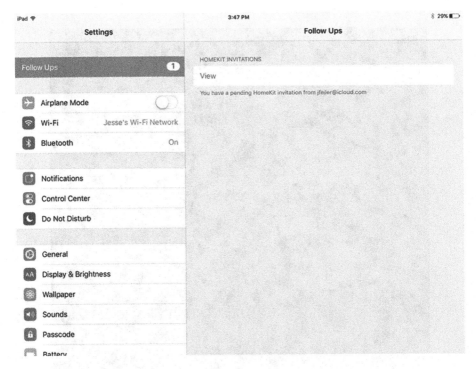

Figure 9-8. The invitee can choose to view the invitation

If the user chooses to see the invitation, the view shown in Figure 9-9 appears. Note that iCloud must be enabled to accept the invitation. Rather than send the user off to check to see if iCloud is enabled, the current setting is shown in Figure 9-9. If it's off, the user can turn it on from here. (The other iCloud settings remain available in Settings.)

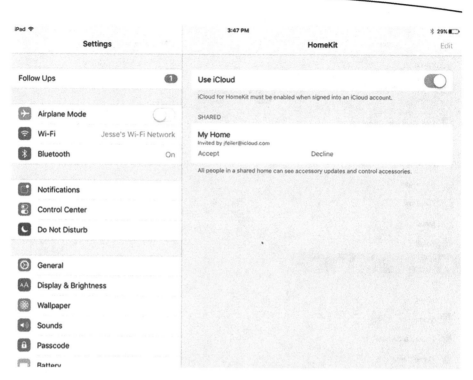

Figure 9-9. The invitee accepts or declines the invitation

If the user accepts, the action is reversible. Just go back to HomeKit in Settings to view the home(s) to which you have access. You can leave any of them as you see in Figure 9-10.

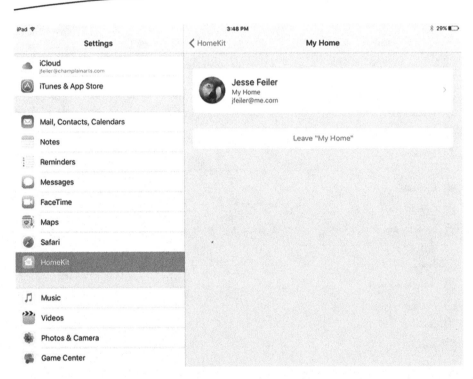

Figure 9-10. *You can leave a home at any time*

> **Tip** If you're going to be inviting people to share your home (perhaps relatives or others in the house who have different Apple IDs), you might want to modify the default My Home name for the home.

Responding on an iPhone

If the invitee views the invitation on an iPhone, here's what it looks like. First of all, HomeKit is still in Settings on iPhone, but it looks a bit different as you see in Figure 9-11. (In this section, a few of the intermediate screens that are identical to iPad are omitted.)

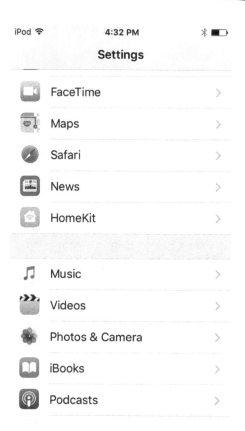

Figure 9-11. *View the invitation on an iPhone*

After choosing to see the invitation (just as on the iPad), the invitee can modify iCloud settings. If the invitee is already part of a home, this is where to come to begin the process of leaving by tapping the relevant home, as you can see in Figure 9-12.

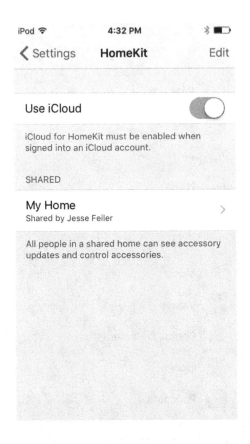

Figure 9-12.

Once you tap the home you're interested in working with, you can leave it as you see in Figure 9-13

Figure 9-13. *Change HomeKit settings on iPhone*

Set Permissions for Users

To set permissions for users, go to the Home tab in the Home app, tap Edit, and then tap the disclosure triangle next to the home name. You'll see the alert shown in Figure 9-14.

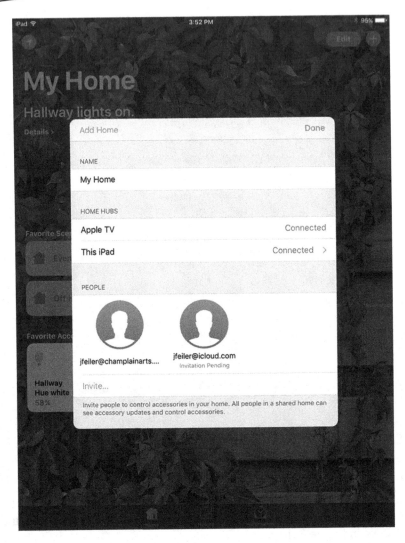

Figure 9-14. Manage users

Note that Figure 9-14 shows two users: one has a pending invitation and the other is already a user. You can invite someone else if you want, as you saw previously in Figure 9-5.

Double-tap a user to set permissions as you can see in Figure 9-15.

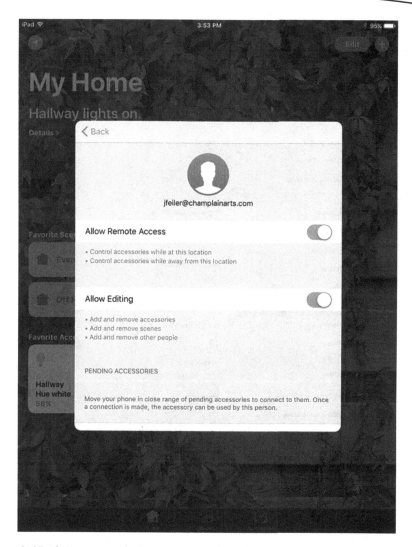

Figure 9-15. Set user permissions

Allowing Lock Screen Access

One final setting may be useful to you and to the people with whom you share a home. In Settings, go to Touch ID & Password, as shown in Figure 9-16, and turn on Home Control (that's HomeKit). If it's set up, Touch ID will work for Home Settings.

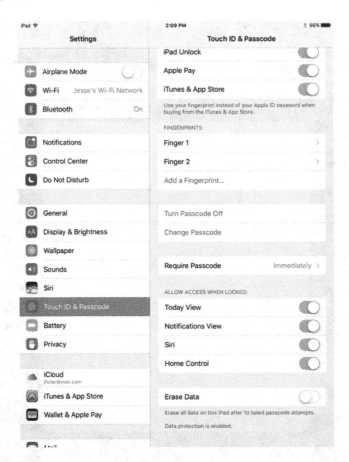

Figure 9-16.   Allow lock screen access

Index

Get the eBook for only $4.99!

Why limit yourself?

Now you can take the weightless companion with you wherever you go and access your content on your PC, phone, tablet, or reader.

Since you've purchased this print book, we are happy to offer you the eBook for just $4.99.

Convenient and fully searchable, the PDF version enables you to easily find and copy code—or perform examples by quickly toggling between instructions and applications.

To learn more, go to http://www.apress.com/us/shop/companion or contact support@apress.com.

Printed in the United States
By Bookmasters